7/12/01
$9.50
B+T

AS

14 Day

11/01

Withdrawn

Sons of the River

DUE

Sons of the River

A Nebraska Memoir

Norm Bomer

Norm Bomer, *Sons of the River: A Nebraska Memoir*
Published by Canon Press, P.O. Box 8729, Moscow, ID 83843
www.canonpress.org
800-488-2034

05 04 03 02 01 00   9 8 7 6 5 4 3 2 1

Cover design by Paige Atwood Design, Moscow, ID
Cover artwork by Carol Bomer
Interior design by Courtney Huntington

Library of Congress Cataloging-in-Publication Data

Bomer, Norm, 1946–
    Sons of the river: a Nebraska memoir/Norm Bomer.
    p. cm.
    ISBN 1-885767-67-6
    1. Bomer, Norm. 2. Farm life—Nebraska—Ewing. 3. Ewing
    (Neb.)—Biography. I. Title
    CT275.B5838 A3 2000
    978.2'745—dc21   00-009413

For the Sons of the Elkhorn

Contents

Time, like an ever rolling stream,
bears all its sons away;
they fly forgotten, as a dream
dies at the op'ning day.

- I -
The First Hole in the Wall

Night is true night in the ranch country that spreads into the Sand Hills south of Ewing. It is night that seems unaware of the glitter of civilization not far away. The heavens are intimate, enveloping the landscape with color and light without veiling the drama of the darkness.

In the summer of Gordie's wedding, this is where Clayton Hoke and I hunted, gliding over undulating hayfields in his white Impala, dancing graceful reels with the haystacks. Our flight was smooth as flute music in the moonlight and quiet as the stubble that whispered under our tires. In those days of our youth, it was always flight away from everything toward some unseen greatness which we never expected to reach.

The saber beams of our headlights slashed the night, occasionally igniting the eyes of coyotes that nested in the tops of the haystacks. Although we shot a few coons out of the high belts of cottonwoods that hemmed the fields, our hunting had an abstract quality. It was the fantasy and freedom of a Nebraska childhood which I relived in this darkness. It was light to me.

In a small wooden box on my dresser is a black-and-white school photograph of a smiling little boy in wire-rimmed glasses. Gordon Shrader, the boy in the picture, was Ralph and Belva Shrader's only son—a farm boy from just beyond the river ridge northeast of Ewing. Gordie was the first boy I met in May of 1952, when the church elders and their families came into town for the housewarming of the parsonage for the new preacher—my father.

11

I kicked a hole in the wall at the head of the stairs that evening. I just kept kicking until both the wallpaper and the plaster were gone, leaving an open arch above the baseboard. I was five and a half and didn't know what else to do to impress a Nebraska farmer of six.

The replacement patch of bare white plaster greeted everyone who climbed those stairs for years afterwards. It's still there after half a century, fossilized under strata of wallpaper.

The house was moved long ago from the center of town to the edge of town, two blocks away. Gordie and I have moved too—from the impetuosity of children to the hardened wisdom of men. The holes we have foolishly kicked into our lives have left more than scars of plaster.

Two little boys are standing silently side by side, each with an arm over the other's shoulder. I see them—I see Gordie and me—as I look back through the ever-rolling stream of our lives. And then the picture grows slowly wider and deeper, for our enduring friendship has given me passage into a story of forgotten people and a posterity that itself teeters on the edge of silence.

- II -
Out to the Farm

The mighty rivers of America have been vulgarized by commerce, glamorized by legend and song. Acts of the national drama have played across their stages. They have determined battles, fostered grand engineering projects, and fomented disasters. The Mississippi, the Missouri, the Columbia, the Ohio, the Hudson. Their histories have flowed into national, even international, identities.

It's likely that a river flows through the life of every American in every generation. In one person the channel may be shallow. In another it may be deep.

A river flows through my life. But it is not numbered among the mighty. It is neither wide nor long, neither a builder of great cities nor an ally of great armies. It has never even irrigated my land or watered my cattle. It skirts the tiny Nebraska town that was my home for only a few of my childhood years—my father's first charge as a young Presbyterian minister. And yet, year after year, the Elkhorn River cuts a channel deep within my soul, shifting and shaping me like its own sand.

It swells and chokes me with memories, then subsides to reveal fragments of driftwood along its banks: a whiney old green pickup parked under the hickory tree beside my North Carolina home; elk horns mounted on the rough bark of my locust bedposts; boots in my closet; a Winchester squirrel gun on my son's bedroom wall; a pair of nineteenth-century spectacles lying dusty on my desk.

The wide sweep of the Elkhorn River Valley can be captured from the high ground two miles west of Shraders'. The Ewing water tower pokes its silver head above the soft green summer of the treetops which billow out and away toward the Nebraska sand hills.

Beneath that vast canopy in May of 1870, just below the juncture of the Elkhorn and its South Fork, fifty-three-year-old James Ewing arrived from Tennessee with his wife, Sabrina, and two daughters. There he unhitched their covered wagon in woods a mile west of what is today the Antelope County line. He soon discovered an old man named Ford camped on the same side of the river a short distance upstream. The fellow had arrived only weeks earlier, and he died within the year.

Near the forks of the river, Ewing built an oak log cabin with a sod roof—the first house in what was officially to become Holt County six years later. And with a pouch of seeds and an ax to pierce the soil, he planted the first field of sod corn in a clearing beside it.

Short, square Calvin Gunter and his wife, Ruth, came by ox team from "Ioway" the following spring, staking a homestead a mile upstream from the Ewings and establishing their new home in a dugout on the river's north bank.

As other settlers began to arrive on the frontier, they agreed to call their community Ford to honor the old man who had so shortly preceded them. The first small and infrequent mail deliveries from Norfolk, fifty miles down river, were brought by stagecoach to the Ewings' log cabin for distribution.

Norfolk was not only the postal railhead; its very name was postal. The original name, Norfork, had been derived from the town's location on the North Fork of the Elkhorn. But when the Post Office Department approved the town's petition for a post office in 1867, it changed the name to "Norfolk" on all documentation.

Federal bureaucrats apparently thought the town fathers couldn't spell. In their desire not to jeopardize their postal status, the chagrined town fathers acquiesced.

That historical anecdote had more than a folklorish effect on the culture. To this day, the town is "Norfork" to the people of the Valley.

When the westward rails of the Fremont, Elkhorn, and Missouri Valley finally crossed the South Fork in 1882, the Ford postal station was transferred from James Ewing's fiddle case to the depot on the edge of the new village across the river. George Butler, the first appointed postmaster, called it Ewing Post Office in honor of his pioneering predecessor.

It wasn't until May 8, 1884 that the village of Ewing was incorporated by authority of county commissioner J.E. West. The new town was, even as it is called today, "Gateway to the Sand Hills," leading the way into the vast landscape of Nebraska's west. James Ewing had indeed opened the gate, driving his stakes a full four years before John O'Neill established the small Irish colony bearing his name—twenty miles further up the Elkhorn.

Before 1876, Holt County, Nebraska, was known by pioneers as Elkhorn County, which was much larger than it is today—16,000 square miles of wilderness. It eventually became ten counties, a vast map marked, even today, with only a few road lines and a smattering of town dots. Elkhorn County reached from the Antelope County line 300 miles across western Nebraska to what later became Wyoming. When the narrower boundaries of Holt County were officially confirmed in January of 1877, the rest was mapped as Unorganized Territory or Indian Territory but remained legally attached to Holt County for judicial and tax purposes. It was the West, the land of *taraha*, the buffalo. It was the hunting ground of the Pawnee, the Ponca, the Omaha, the Cheyenne, and the Sioux.

"The Indian who gazed down the Elkhorn Valley must have thought that here indeed was the playground of the gods, the true Happy Hunting Ground," read an article in the September 6, 1884 edition of the magazine *The Leading Industries of the West*. "The hollow was governed by quiet and serenity and adorned by magnificent trees, green, green grasses turning to gold in the August sunshine, blue skies and a shining river winding crazily from one end of the world to the other, with branches making an unorthodox pattern over the entire countryside."

It was that antlerish pattern which had inspired French Canadian trappers of the late eighteenth century to name the river *Corne de Cerf* (Horn of the Elk). Were geographical names part of the creation itself, however, the name Elkhorn County would have seemed only natural. The Elkhorn River was the lifeblood of the valley, giving vitality not just to a land but also to a people.

Its native cottonwood, white elm, ash, oak, and willow provided lumber and fuel. Wild plums, chokecherries, grapes, gooseberries, and wild asparagus flourished by its side. So did elk, white-tailed deer, wild turkey, beaver, and quail. And reaching out along the Elkhorn's many tributary streams were clusters of hackberry, box elder, linden, and basswood.

"There is no more beautiful prairie country in the world," wrote painter George Catlin in 1832.

From the banks of the river the valley ascended as much as 500 feet, sometimes gradually, sometimes abruptly. The bluffs and rolling prairie beyond the trees were thick with native grasses like blue joint and wild oats, rich forage for the buffalo and the prong-horn antelope and eventually for the livestock of pioneers. Prairie chickens and sharp-tailed grouse nested there in abundance.

On February 21, 1872, James Ewing's oldest

daughter, Anna Davidson, seventeen, bore a son—the first white child born in Elkhorn County. On April 15, James Gunter, who was delivered in Calvin and Ruth's dugout just up the river, became the second.

I entered the Gunter home three generations later, where short, square Lionel Gunter and his wife, Martha, were raising a covey of handsome, soft-spoken sons—Calvin Gunter's great-grandsons. A two-story frame farmhouse had long since replaced the dugout, the subsequent log cabin, and the original frame house which had burned down at the turn of the century.

When I was a child, my father occasionally drove our family north from Ewing on the county road, across the old bridge, then down a long driveway through a cornfield and into trees where the Gunter house stood. I remember a Sunday afternoon when he parked our '50 Ford on the shaded barnyard among the chickens. Lionel told us it would be fine if we wanted to leave it there and walk on south through the trees with our picnic lunch.

Bill Bomer was the preacher, after all. The people of the upper Elkhorn Valley gave him genuine veneration and sometimes charity—which came amiably wrapped for my dad, a city boy fresh out of seminary like a loaf hot out of the oven.

That heat generated some righteous steam which, on a particular Sunday morning in his first year, he had let off with a sermon about Sabbath observance. He thumped his pulpit and delineated the relevant sins under each of two sub-points, sins of omission and sins of commission. The latter category included such things as milking cows and gathering eggs on the Lord's day.

A few days later, he made a pastoral call on one of his rural flock who happened to be tossing some eggs out of a chicken coop—eggs that had obviously not been gathered in timely fashion. Their color more resembled Nebraska storm clouds than white fairweather ones.

"This is the way the preacher likes 'em," the farmer announced with a gleam in his eye. The seminary of the farm.

It was Sunday again as we now walked through the grove south of Gunters' house, where Mother spread the picnic blanket by the Elkhorn. I tossed sticks into the water, and my little brother tried to imitate. I was six. Bruce was three. As ants crawled across our blanket during the meal, we all discussed ant behavior and its lessons about work, and then Daddy explained why going on a picnic on the Lord's day wasn't really a violation of the Fourth Commandment. But, he suggested, we probably shouldn't talk about it around anyone from church.

I remember too the tin pail under the sink in Martha Gunter's kitchen. It was full of arrowheads from the cornfield at the corner. Lionel told me the place had been an Indian battleground, and I was enthralled. Describing it as the site of an Omaha hunting camp along the river would have been a bit humdrum by contrast. As in all boys, my imagination helped write the script of the play in which I acted. But my life in that isolated culture really was filled with adventure. I lived on the Elkhorn. I was Gordon Shrader's best friend. Sioux braves, having come to steal Pawnee ponies, were lurking in the trees—or might have been.

As I stand above the river today where James Gunter, Lionel's father, once gazed out over hundreds of Ponca teepees, my imagination contributes to the script in another sense. For the players I see along the Elkhorn are all real, and my imagination is memory.

- III -
Adventures of a Good Boy

The road slopes immediately down to the west from Ralph Shrader's old place at the corner. Gordie used to ride his bicycle down that hill a quarter mile to Grandma Shrader's with Tuffy bobbing behind him on the blur of his stubby legs.

The tool shop was down there. So was the old gable-roofed barn with the horse stalls, the milking shed, and the sow pens. Ralph spent a lot of working hours at Grandma's. It was still like home to him. He had grown up in the brittle old white house on the south side of the road. And now his brittle old mother sat inside rocking with her blanket, even in the summer.

Gordie often rode his bike back and forth to Grandma Shrader's. It was especially exciting the year he got a speedometer. He could pedal that old one-speed down the hill hard enough to make the needle nibble at the thirty. He had to stay on the hard middle of the narrow road. Otherwise, his wheels would get bogged down in the deep sand along the edges, and the wide rubber tires would become studded with sand-burs.

There were trees—mostly gone now—big cotton-wood trees rising like castle towers along both sides of the road. Their high masses of leaves chattered softly in the summer breeze. On some lonely afternoons, they sounded like the rushing waters of a stream following the treetops west down to the Elkhorn River.

In the fenced yard around Ralph's small square house stood dark, fat elms—gone now, like Ralph himself. They kept it in shade all day long. Under their protection the grass grew thick and cool through the hot summers, and the lilacs reached almost to the eaves.

North of the house, across the road, grew a wide grove of cottonwood, mulberry, box elder, and black walnut—a very old grove, where the ground had never been broken by a plow. It followed the road west to the bottom of the hill across from Grandma Shrader's.

During the day, shiny skinks wriggled along the moist sand under logs. An occasional bull snake nudged its way through from the cornfields. Bright-winged grasshoppers clicked from weed to weed, cicadas rasped in the branches, and woodpeckers chiseled away at the bark.

At night, great horned owls emerged from the trees to hunt. Occasionally the trill of a bobcat answered the owls' hooting, and skittish coyotes padded along the borders of the grove, sniffing the sandy soil.

Some days, young Gordie would lay his bike in the hot sand along the road and crawl through the barbed wire fence. There in the woods he would find Nubbins standing still and black in the shade, whisking horseflies with his tail. Gordie would smack the horse on the neck and reach high to give his long face a shake. "Ol' Nubbins! Ol' Nubbins!" he'd repeat fondly through his teeth.

There were times when he'd bring the bridle from Grandma's barn and hang it on a fence post while he crawled through the wires. To put the bridle on, he'd pull Nubbins' head down low and yell at him a few times to keep it down. Then with the thick leather reins in hand, he'd lead the tall horse through the trees to the nearest cottonwood log. He'd climb up on the smooth, white wood, leap hard against Nubbins, and scramble up on his back.

At seven years old, Gordie had already been riding bareback for years. There had been a time when his little legs hardly reached beyond the plateau of Nubbins' wide back. But he stayed on just the same, galloping up the road from Grandma's wearing a quite grownup expression beneath his wire-rimmed glasses. His legs stuck straight out to each side, flapping up and down like the wings of a blue jay.

Nubbins had worked the rodeo in his younger days. He seemed to recall a certain skill from one of the events, for he frequently insisted on turning to the left. But Gordie was a Nebraska farm boy. Even when he was small, he didn't take any guff from a horse.

To little boys like us, Nubbins was a behemoth. Although Gordie and I were the same age and size, I looked up to my friend emotionally the way I looked up to Nubbins physically. Those were glorious occasions, those times when I was invited "out to the farm"—all of five miles from town. Horses always grazed in the secret pasture of my longings—horses waiting to be roped and ridden hard. There were countless other hopes and fears and adventures to be had. But for this preacher's boy from Ewing, nothing—not swimming in the stock tank, not jumping barefoot from the rafters of the wooden granary into the coolness of shelled corn—measured up to riding horseback.

In the earliest years, I sat right in the saddle behind Gordie with my arms folded tightly around his chest. Then Nubbins would trot out of Grandma Shrader's barnyard and break, slow-motion, into a rolling lope. I was wonderfully frightened of falling off, yet always encouraged by Gordie's offhand dominion over Nubbins.

By the time we were seven, I had graduated to behind the saddle, grasping the cantle desperately as we galloped over what seemed like tidal waves. At noon, we'd head up the road to Gordie's, sometimes slapping Nubbins with the reins to outrun Ralph in his whiney old green International pickup. We were captivated by the smooth power of that black horse beneath us, and for a short time between the shelter belts of cottonwood, we were men.

- IV -
A Picnic at the River

The sturdy preaching which strode into the small semicircle of wooden pews around my father's first pulpit was gradually informed by the eternal truths of agriculture. In other words, Daddy's fervent orthodoxy grew less and less academic as he better understood the rotten egg realities of farming.

His earliest hellfire sermons about Sabbath observance, for example, were fine-tuned both by the Scriptures and the created order of things. Christ's pointed approval of pulling oxen from wells on the Sabbath gained rich new meaning as Daddy personally came to know bawling dairy cows created to be milked on all seven days of the week.

At the same time, the eternal truths of the Scriptures bore fruit in the earthly harvests of the people. And their demonstrations of gratitude went far beyond the generous salary that climbed in three years to $300 a month. We were regularly blessed with gifts of sweet corn, cream, eggs, garden vegetables, and bakery.

At my age, I didn't appreciate my father's preaching in quite the same way as did the adults of the congregation. But I did appreciate the singular aspects that applied to me. "And if Norman will put down his Sunday school paper, I'm sure he'll get something out of today's sermon too," are the only words I remember from the pulpit during those three years at the Ewing Presbyterian Church. So in a way, I guess he was right.

The people I remember—men with dark leather faces and pale foreheads; women with velvety veiled hats and sympathetic eyes; boys with burr haircuts and diaphanous pastel shirts; girls with high curls and wide skirts.

I also remember the personal object lessons on re-demption which I received both through punishment and forgiveness. The former was delivered with a bit of that same hellfire enthusiasm that inspired Daddy's preaching.

On one such emotional occasion, I blurted out that I was afraid to do something wrong for fear he'd "throw me through the wall or something." That phrase be-came a sort of family motto. "Better not do that, or Daddy might just throw you through the wall again," my mother would say. At the supper table, I would rib my dad about how he always "threw me through the wall." Years later, my little brother would say, "Remem-ber how Daddy used to throw you through the wall?"

When I was in my teens, Mother did admit that she felt my early punishments had been a little severe—at least much more severe than those subsequently re-ceived by my younger brother and sister. But, she said, that's probably why I "turned out so good." The "so good" was a combination of motherly pride and wishful thinking. The fruits of my life were not always so good or so prudent, as I frequently demonstrated even during my young Tom Sawyerish days in Ewing.

Shorty's Shoe Shop was behind a narrow door on the west end of Main Street. It was the final stop on the small boys' slingshot circuit. First stop was any tree in Ewing that would yield the appropriate crotch of a small limb. Second stop was the Firestone store for a dis-carded inner tube—made of real rubber in those days. The next stop was Shorty's for a piece of leather just the right size and thickness for a slingshot pouch.

Shorty was a midget who sat on a high wooden bench in front of his sewing machine. There wasn't much room in the small shop for anything else. We'd squeeze inside the door, and Shorty would happily slide down and open the lid of the bench to reveal his stash of leather scraps. We loved the aroma and the rich colors of the leather. And we felt secure with Shorty, for he knew slingshots and his stature made him seem a little more like us than the other adults in town. He'd trim our selected pieces and punch holes in the corners where we could attach the strips of inner tube.

For a boy in old Ewing, carrying a slingshot in the back pocket was as important as carrying a Barlow knife in the front. My friends and I shot rocks at the sides of garages and barns, tree trunks, telephone poles, wash tubs, tin cans, stray cats, birds on wires, and birds in trees. We also shot rocks at water. From the banks of the Elkhorn, we'd target carp and floating sticks. In the swamps, we'd shoot at bullfrogs when their heads bumped up through the green scum of the duckweed. Sometimes we'd just shoot to hear the *gla-roomp* and see the splash.

One day, Larry Shilosky and I got bored with the usual targets and decided to try some man-to-man combat. I climbed into the haymow of the little barn behind his little house next door to the Methodist Church. Larry stayed below. The battle was brief. When I leaned out of the open haymow door for recon, Larry was waiting at the corner of the open barn door below—with his weapon loaded and cocked. He let fly with a rock the diameter of a quarter. It was a superb shot which hit me directly in the eye.

My screaming brought Larry's mom into the backyard on a dead run, where she immediately diverted my attention by taking the stoutest slingshot I had ever made and snapping it in two with her bare hands. I was so shocked by her brute strength and summary judgment that I cried all the harder. The pain of the broken slingshot hurt more than the pain of the broken eye.

The further reward for my lack of prudence was a frantic trip with my parents to Clearwater ten miles away where the last of the country doctors still kept shop. His one-room office wasn't much bigger than Shorty's. The old man squeaked around on his swivel chair when we entered and then pulled back a curtain to reveal his examining room—a high, firmly padded table against the wall. I went home with a good prognosis and a proud patch taped over my eye. My little brother was green with envy.

There were other escapades that could have led to worse consequences. Before we were seven, my classmate Terry Wright and I had tired of smoking grapevine out by the river and decided to try something more sophisticated. We each carried a paper bag down to Main Street and collected the best cigarette butts we could find along the sidewalk. Then we climbed into the barn across the alley behind his tiny house for a real smoke.

I never found out who called my mom, but the minute I got home, I knew someone had. I sat with her on the living room couch and made one of my life's hardest confessions—that I had courted demon tobacco. Daddy was in the yard polishing the car, and I was stricken with terror knowing that he would soon be giving me the severest polishing of my life. Then I was surprised by grace.

Mother saw the terror in me and must have felt a little of it herself, for she agreed not to tell him. The offense was serious enough that I would have been thrown through the wall, and neither of us was up to it. I promised I would never do such a thing again, and I kept that promise for a number of months—a long time for a good kid my age.

- V -
Shraders and
a Frontier Legacy

At twelve sharp, the siren on the water tower in Ewing sounded long and loud. The tower stood beside the alley not far from the backyard of the parsonage. For us town boys, sitting on our bikes directly under it at noon was a rite of fraternity. We threw our elbows in the air and smashed our ears shut with our palms as the siren pummeled us from above.

It was unnerving to imagine that the disorienting attack of noise might not end. But it was somehow gratifying that for a brief moment all other threats to our small world were shut out by the noise. So were inequalities among us that seemed large in our little lives. Suddenly we were all tongue-tied like tongue-tied Terry. And suddenly crazy Lonnie was no crazier than the rest of us screaming with laughter.

When the air was right, the siren could be heard faintly out on the Shrader farm. But it wasn't lunch time on the farm. The noon meal was called dinner.

On the select days when I was there to ride the horse home for dinner, Gordie and I tied him to a leg of the windmill or, on hotter days, to a shady willow beside the chicken coop. Like most Nebraska chicken coops in those early fifties, it was really just a roosting shed. The Shrader chickens weren't egg machines confined to wire baskets. The laying hens were able to nest in open shelf boxes along the front wall of the coop. And they were free to spend their days texturing the barnyard with their peckings and scratchings and leavings.

Belva insisted on keeping the gate into the house yard shut against the chickens. We were usually greeted at the kitchen door with affectionate threatening reminders. And if we left the gate open on our way out after dinner, we never got out of range before Belva's stern "Gor-DON!" rang out, rising an octave from the first syllable to the second.

Belva was an articulate woman with a commanding stature and a massive wood-burning cookstove. I loved her because she was my best friend's mom and because she was Belva Shrader, kind, stern, and constant. I was awed by the fact that she had been a schoolteacher and amazed by her courage, for she stuck insulin needles into her own legs every day.

It seemed to take so much to be the woman of the farm. I sensed even then what a high calling it was to be Ralph Shrader's godly wife and Gordie's faithful mom. I did not sense in what direction we were all moving in our earthly glory. Then so many years later, I saw her in her house in town, living alone, frail and slow, heartfull of memories, sitting on the old couch with her Bible in her lap. And then, not at all.

Belva's kitchen was on the southwest corner of the farmhouse. We'd let the creaky screen door slap shut behind us as we clomped across the linoleum past the hand pump on the long porcelain sink, past counters of fresh white bread rolls and Mason jars of apple butter, around the iron stove, and into the bathroom just past the open pantry door. There before dinner we washed our hands with Lava soap. It made me feel like a farmer and a Shrader. We used smooth, white soap at our house in town. Town folks, I figured, didn't need things like Lava soap and iron stoves and bullwhips.

When Ralph came in to wash his hands, I liked to

hang around and watch. He always plugged the sink and let it fill like a bathtub while he rolled up the sleeves of his blue work shirt. Then his brown hands worked that Lava bar over his white forearms like a plow working virgin prairie. The water turned so dark I never could understand how he could keep washing in it. But he did—even splashing his face and rubbing the back of his neck with water. And then he opened his jackknife and plowed some more under his fingernails. It was a ritual of a strong man, such a ritual just to eat dinner.

When we were so young, dinnertime on the farm was a mildly tedious interruption of adventure. Wash hands, sit at the table, exercise good manners, and later be quiet for a short nap time. None of it was painful, of course. In fact, my invitations to the farm were fairly infrequent, so even the tedious was better than home tedious.

Dinner began with prayers of thanksgiving, usually offered by Belva instead of Ralph. I thought it a bit curious, being used to hearing my father lead prayers at our table at home, even though my mother was up to the task when he wasn't there. Out in the working world of the farm, Ralph wasn't timid about pointing out "what the good Lord saw fit to do" or "how the good Lord made it" or, in later years, that "the good Lord had a purpose" in taking his leg in a farm accident. But publicly asking God's blessing of the table usually fell to Belva. She did, after all, spend more time in the house where the Bible was. And she had prepared the food.

Ralph assumed prominent roles of leadership in the church. But his short repertoire in spiritual administration at home seemed in some way to prolong the legacy of his own father, who had never followed Grandma Shrader to church even as a social exercise. Albert Shrader had been a good provider who fed cattle, raised pigs, chewed tobacco, and peppered his eggs. But he had pretty much left his life unsalted.

After dinner, Gordie was expected to lie down in his bed, and I was given Ralph and Belva's bed just off the living room. We couldn't take our "naps" together, since we had a giggle problem that even exacerbated as we got older. Ralph was the only one who actually slept. In the years when he still had both his legs, he'd flop flat out on the living room rug and dream about horses. I don't know that for a fact. But I imagine Ralph was like me in that respect, although he was unlike me in another. He was a real horseman.

I was captivated by Ralph's stories of the early days when he had used horses to work the farm and had actually ridden them on business. The stories weren't so far removed from my experience as to seem like fairy tales. A few of the old-timers still hadn't changed all that much in the isolated world of the upper Elkhorn Valley. Angular old Nellie Conner occasionally drove her horse-drawn lumber wagon into town with her sister, angular old Sarah Hohman from the Biddlecome farm out by the river. The sheriff, when we had one, made her park it beside the post office on the side street, for it was too long to park on Main Street without blocking traffic.

Nellie Conner's place was east of Biddlecomes' on the river ridge up past Gunters'. Nellie's late husband, Oliver, had once left a Model-T in a shed there, a major investment of $393 in 1916. Nellie never touched that exotic thing. She harbored it in the shed for years after his death, then sold it during the Depression—five bucks for scrap.

Like Nellie, Sarah was more at home behind a team than behind a steering wheel. Once, long ago, there had also been an automobile sitting idle in the huge barn at her place—a Cord brought home by her younger brother George. It was more exotic even than the Ford—too exotic for the Elkhorn Valley. In those difficult years before her father's death in the early thirties, Sarah gave in to scalpers one day and let it go for a few dollars.

Sometimes Sarah passed our house alone with her own team and buggy—the same buggy she had driven to town in the teens of the century with her two young daughters—Phyllis on her lap and Lucille standing behind the seat.

Now in Sarah's old age, her eldest daughter, Lucille, had become Biddlecome by name and so had the Hohman farm. But the Hohman pioneers still had a presence in every corner. In the northwest parlor of the big barn, the old buggy, that fine old buggy, still sat in the dusty shadows, Landau irons and all. The weathered wooden shed next to the stone coop west of the house was piled and hung wall to wall with Adam Hohman's handmade furniture and handmade tools from the early homestead. Twig chairs and limb-legged tables lay tilted in cobweb and dirt. They were decorated with crooked scythes and bow saws and draw knives honed and hammered from iron strap. In one corner stood the bellows from his blacksmith business—the first in the county.

The pioneers themselves were gone now, yet few signs of modern America were apparent in the venerable Ewing, Nebraska, of the early fifties. Anomalies of geography and circumstance had kept this very old and very small window open to the past. But travelers on the state highway never saw the still-living American frontier as they went speeding by.

This had been Indian country, part of vast hunting grounds skirted even by nineteeth-century pioneer commerce and by what later became known as progress. One of the lesser of the Mormon Trails had followed the Elkhorn through here. But the Oregon, California, and primary Mormon Trails had traversed Nebraska Territory further south along the natural highway of the Platte Valley, where the Pawnee had built their permanent earth-lodge villages.

Nebraska north of the Platte was described by early explorers as little more than windblown dune sand and prairie grass, a barren wasteland to be avoided by pioneers. On his 1796 exploration map, Collot labeled it simply "Barren Country Composed of Chalk, Sand, and Gravel." It lacked the timber and water necessary for settlement—a hostile landscape rife with hostile savages.

In 1819, the U.S. government sent a twenty-two-man expedition under the command of a Major Long to explore the Platte Valley. The company sailed the *Western Engineer* from Pittsburgh, down the Ohio, up the Mississippi, and up the Missouri to the Council Bluff. No steamboat had ever before gone as far as Nebraska.

The party wintered west of the river where Omaha would later emerge. In June, Major Long and twenty-one other men struck out toward the Rockies on horseback. On June 11, they mounted a ridge at the Loup River and saw stretching away before them a ten-mile sweep of earth lodges housing 6,000 Pawnees. In his later report, Long provided an accurate account of Indians and their customs but did less of a service to the reputation of Nebraska itself. With words that would someday be erased by reality, he wrote, "It is almost wholly unfit for cultivation and, of course, uninhabitable for people depending upon agriculture for their subsistence."

In the 1840s, writer Rufus Sage expressed a similar assessment of the western three-fourths of Nebraska, "That this section of the country should ever become inhabited by civilized man . . . is an idea too preposterous to be entertained for a single moment."

Washington Irving called it "irreclaimable wilderness."

In the mid-1800s, Olney's widely-used school geography text built upon the myth, succinctly labeling

Nebraska Territory the "Great American Desert." Whether or not it was truly uninhabitable, the perennial truth was that it remained widely uninhabited—the Western frontier.

Even into the second decade of the twentieth century, the nineteenth century survived largely intact in the upper Elkhorn Valley and the Sand Hills to the west. By the time of my childhood, significant remnants of the frontier still survived, not only in the old people but in the culture itself.

Charlie Good, the dray man, still regularly drove his team of Belgians down to Main Street for supplies. As he came by the parsonage, I would run into the sandy street and jump on the back of his freight wagon to ride to the feed store with the other kids he'd already collected along the way.

While Ralph the horseman snoozed in the living room, I listened to the hog feeders clink down by the barn.

- VI -
Going to Town

Gordie might have had some desire to taste a preacher's kid's life in a town of 720 souls, with a water tower, a movieshow, and the Elkhorn—river of unlimited adventure. But it never became obvious. It certainly never rivaled my fadeless love for the farm.

When I was five, I asked my mom after a church supper to ask his mom if he could stay overnight with me. That was the end of our raucous playing for that evening. He cried quietly and stuck close to Belva until they got into Ralph's Ford and drove home. I figured that was my answer.

The needs of Gordie's world seldom extended as far as town, five miles away. In his childhood, it was a world far smaller than the isolated one of his father. Here at the meeting of Holt and Antelope Counties the Elkhorn Valley of the early 1950s was in many respects only approaching the borders of modernity. A man's farm was a man's country, and "town" was his world's sole base of commerce.

A farmer listened to the daily markets with a keen ear for livestock and corn. But his free enterprise remained microcosmic. With open tractor and wagon, he hauled his shelled corn to the same local elevators year after year. Seeking better markets outside the small circle would have broached a culture.

During the week, town was the grain elevator, sale barn, creamery, implement dealer, bank, lumber yard, railroad depot, and, on very rare occasion, cafe. It was also the blacksmith shop, the school, and the beer joints. Ralph Shrader patronized the blacksmith only seldom, the school and bars not at all. Except for the most complicated machinery breakdowns, Ralph's blacksmithing was done at the shop back by the glass-top gas pump on Grandma Shrader's yard. As for drinking, he adjudged it to be unchristian and beer joints somehow worse than that. The schooling of his two children was done at the one-room schoolhouse that he himself had attended just beyond the willow grove west of the shop.

Since the schoolhouse was only a stone's throw beyond Grandma's, it was close enough for Gordie and his older sister, Dianne, to walk or ride their bikes the quarter mile from Ralph's corner. In fair weather, some of the other students rode horses, and even Gordie sometimes tied Nubbins in the shade beside Clayton Hoke's pony, Smokey. After school, he and Clayton would gallop together up and down the road, then finally slow their horses to a trot as they headed west past Uncle Wilbur Bennett's place to the corner. There Clayton would turn south into the narrow, shaded road to his home a mile away—the same road his father, Dewitt, had followed home from the same schoolhouse every afternoon when the century was in its teens. Back then, the road had been just a grassy lane between shelter belts planted by the first settlers with switches from cottonwoods down by the river.

For a short distance, Clayton would run Smokey full bore until he was sure Gordie had heard the echoes of his speed. Then he'd mosey the rest of the way, watching for deer and raccoon tracks in the sand and sometimes picturing the Gypsies who had camped there with their covered wagons long ago when his dad and the road were both still green.

The Gypsies back then would graze their horses for days and beg bread and potatoes and eggs from Grandma Hoke, same as the Omahas had done from their teepee camps along the Elkhorn when she had been a young girl and a Gunter.

Not all valley farm wives in those days, however, took a cotton to the Gypsies. Belva Shrader recalled that when she was a young girl, her mother was terrified of them. The mysterious Gypsy women were always wrapped in large shawls. "You didn't know what was under them," Belva remembered. Perhaps it was chickens, for dozens of them disappeared from local farms whenever the Gypsies came through.

Clayton Hoke knew something about Gypsies too, as did I, for in the early fifties, they still came out of nowhere in their ragtag caravans of cars and trucks, camping at the edge of town, then heading into nowhere again. By then, however, the Indians along the upper Elkhorn were present only in the arrowheads turned up by cultivator shovels and in the traces of the Pawnee graves found in the bluffs above Biddlecomes' place— graves plundered in 1905 by the work crew digging clay for the new road north of Ewing.

After leaving Clayton at the corner, Gordie would lope back east a mile for Belva's cookies and milk, then return to Grandma's for chores, trotting Nubbins from the barn and out the south lane to bring in the cows. To his young way of thinking, life was to do man's work on the farm—a proposition far less fearful and fascinating than to spend a night in town with a preacher's kid who lived on the exotic fringe of society as it should be.

For the farm families of the Elkhorn Valley, "town" of week's end meant much more than commerce. Saturday night in Ewing was county fair, summer vacation, and Fourth of July in one weekly package. Cars from the local farms and from the remote ranches of the Sand Hills to the southwest angled up to the high sidewalks on both sides of the wide, sandy Main Street. And they even huddled two-deep up the middle. Unlike today, pickups weren't considered worthy for Saturday nights or Sunday mornings either one. They stayed on the farm with the implements and the dirty clothes.

On each side of the street for one block the lights of the stores blazed into the night. Women crisscrossed the street, laughing and chatting about their families and about the latest products in Pollocks' dry goods store or Hill's Variety. They carried groceries from the Red & White or the K-B Market and exchanged delightful words with the men gathered in clusters on the street and on the benches in front of the stores.

They took charitable shifts lingering in ancient Mrs. Eggelston's curiosity shop, which was quaintly cluttered with ribbons, thimbles, China darning dolls, tortoiseshell hair combs, trivets, and one of everything not really needed. "I have just the one," Mrs. Eggelston feebly told any customer who feigned interest in one of her singular treasures: a China squirrel, a button tin, a one-inch pocket knife, a peacock brooch, a blue lamp-chimney. She spoke deliberately, pointing a finger and ducking her head slightly away from her lifted hand.

Kids dodged among the parked cars, spending nickels on ice cream cones from Gibsons' Drug Store and candy from K-B's. There Bob the butcher grinned busily from behind the lighted meat case at the back of the store while up front Kermit winked at us over the top of his glasses and gave affectionate discounts on the penny candy.

Up the block to the west, Slim Harris stood beside his red popcorn cart, filling the street with that gay aroma and dispensing riddles and white bags of popcorn to the kids. They passed in excited clumps on various great adventures, sharing the best of them with Slim. And so he heard, with various interpretations throughout the evening, of the dead cat in the alley or the mysterious car parked behind the telephone office.

Down the block to the east, Randolph Scott, my favorite movie cowboy, was bringing even more great adventure to town. After all, it was Saturday night. The Eldorado Theater was open.

On Sunday morning, most of the families streamed back into town with another, more subdued, excitement, distributing their cars among the several churches. For there was open recognition, and not just on Sunday, that the Elkhorn Valley was ultimately not autonomous at all. Assembling to worship the Lord of the wide world was no less essential than cultivating the corn in the summer or shelling it in the winter. On Sunday, Main Street was empty.

At the white Presbyterian church, my father stood in the pulpit, and Ralph Shrader's family sat shoulder to shoulder in dark wood pews with Spanglers and Biddlecomes and Johnstons and Gunters and various other Shraders. Each week, Ralph's plump sister Luella Bennett was at the piano up front, playing with faith in large measure and finesse in smaller dimensions. In sickness or in health, in plenty or in want, the members of the congregation sang their praises with robust devotion. For they were people of hope. The blessing of work was truly seen as blessing, even through the years of affliction.

In the best of years, dry land farming in the sandy soil was only moderately productive. In one particular season, Ralph had to plant the same field four times. The crop either burned up or grasshoppers got it. The words of the apostle were the unwritten inscription on the door posts of the people's houses and barns: "For our light affliction, which is but for a moment, worketh for us a far more exceeding and eternal weight of glory."

It was not merely a simple faith so often attributed to a simple people. It was a theology of the obvious. For in his greatest demonstration of power, the Lord himself had embraced the cross. The power of God wasn't demonstrated in the full ear of corn only, but also in the affliction of hail and drought, locust and worm.

Gordie was a man when he came to understand that reality in his heart of hearts. For it was through bitter years of hostility between them—the greatest affliction of their lives—that he and Ralph Shrader at last came to terms with the love of a father and son.

- VII -
Three Cowboys

We moved from Nebraska to Oklahoma in 1955. But my child's heart never left the Elkhorn Valley—even when challenged.

In the first year after our leaving, I was shocked into a moment of maturity one day in my fourth grade classroom in Oklahoma City. My most beloved teacher, Mrs. Mooy, a large widow-lady in a navy dress, was teaching us the glories of Oklahoma history. But my mind was two states north. "I still like Ewing better," I said aloud, having intimated as much on previous occasions.

"Ewing" was a catch-all term for swimming in the Elkhorn, catching sliders in the swamps, cane-pole fishing for blue gills and bullheads, and making bale forts in hay mows. It meant riding Charlie Good's dray wagon and going midnight coon hunting in Dutch Spangler's Model A. It meant jumping into bins of vetch or corn until my bare feet were raw. And, of course, it meant Gordie.

Had Mrs. Mooy been a violent widow-lady in a navy dress, she would have hurt part of my nine-year-old body. That might have been faster healing then the injury she did inflict verbally that day upon my nine-year-old ego in the presence of my peers. It was about time I faced the fact that this was her beloved Oklahoma and that she was through hearing about Ewing, period.

In the summer of 1957, when I was ten, my parents put me on the Chicago Northwestern in Omaha, and I rode a coach the 180 miles to the Ewing station, my forehead against a window framing the cottonwoods and corn along the Elkhorn. After we passed Clearwater station, I could see the distant silver water tower rising from the dark line of trees that was Ewing.

Under the tower, I could see myself "napping" in the upstairs bedroom of the gamble-roof parsonage beside the Presbyterian church, listening to the harmonies of cicadas and turtle doves and watching puffs of seed drift from the cottonwoods in Ina Bennett's yard. In the mindflow of the past, I could see myself counting boxelder bugs on the hot cement in front of the Eldorado. I could see myself after a summer rain, catching polliwogs in the long puddle that regularly formed under the elms in front of the church. I could see myself on Gordie's farm five miles out across the river.

Ralph and Belva and Gordie were standing on the depot platform in Sunday clothes when the train clanked to a stop. I had planned to say "y'all" upon arrival. But by the time I plopped clumsily down the iron steps, I had abandoned my childish airs of Oklahoma sophistication in the rail car, and on they went with the train past the sale barn and off west towards O'Neill and Valentine.

Neither Gordie nor I knew quite what to say as we climbed into the back seat of Ralph's car. The little boys we had been had passed away in the intervening two years, and we were now little strangers unprepared for the confusion of our lives. The reality of it filled the seat between us, bare in the sunlight. We didn't know each other, and we didn't understand why. But the awkwardness for me was no match for the joy of being headed "out to the farm," where horses always grazed in the secret pasture of my longings—horses waiting to be roped and ridden hard.

Gordie, at eleven, was a young man in active

contrast to my boyness. He now rode ol' Nubbins as much for work bringing the cows in from pasture in late afternoon as for pleasure. He now drove big tractors by himself, cultivating the sandy cornfields with the International M and even pulling wagonloads of corn five miles to the elevator in Orchard. I sat against the fender beside him, awestruck by his skill and responsibility. Sometimes I joined him in the wide steel seat, proud to be the personal friend of a farmer.

I had come back longing to rediscover the Elkhorn Valley of my childhood imagination. Instead I discovered the Elkhorn Valley of deeper substance, tasting the grit and glory of the last generation of Americans to embrace the land in the isolation and security of their frontier heritage.

It wasn't until 1961, four years later, that I returned again to the Elkhorn for a few short weeks that were to become long weeks in my memory. By 1961, Gordie and I were even more apparently different people. Two skinny little boys had become two skinny big boys with interests reaching into the wider community—namely the teenage girls for whom, we agreed, neither of us qualified. About all we had to show for our fourteen years were cracking voices and the tender, swollen nipples of masculine puberty.

There were definite advantages to being unencumbered by actual romantic relationships, even though imaginary ones did occupy frequent parts of our conversation. In lieu of real women, we had real horses. They weren't those horses of my childhood dreams. There was no Randolph-Scott roping to be done. But one day I found out they could be ridden hard.

On that day, Gordie rode a tall sorrel mare named Angel, and I was allotted the safer back of ol' Nubbins. At the corner west of Bennetts', we turned south on the old Gypsy road to pick up Clayton Hoke—my first personal contact with the boy who would someday become my close friend. With Clayton on Smokey, we headed south from the Hoke place and on toward the Elkhorn. We could have chosen a route west to the river, for it runs through the valley in a southeasterly direction. But it wouldn't have taken us past farms where young women might have been watching from porches.

A mile and a half south of the Hokes', we opened a barbed wire gate and rode west across a rolling pasture and into the woods. The horses' hooves whump-whumped against the sandy earth as they flickered through dim shafts of light, strode over mossy hack-berry logs, and shied around tangles of wild raspberry. At the brow of the river bluff, we reined them north-westerly down across the wooded slope and then out over the hot river sand. We finally broke through a thick row of sandbar willows and slide-stepped the horses down the soft bank and into the river.

The dark flood waters of late spring had passed, leaving towering jams of bleached cottonwoods at bends and snags along the high banks. In some places, piles of woody debris lay far back from the water across wide flats of white sand. The river was now shallow, wandering instead of charging toward the Platte and on to the Missouri. In the wider parts, it felt its way along with clear fingers separated by long sandbars and small islands.

The legs of our jeans were soaked by the splash of the horses. We ate wild mulberries from overhanging branches and ogled the still side channels for turtles, river clams, and water snakes. Clayton and I climbed up into the tree jams. Gordie demurred, having a par-ticular aversion to all categories of Nebraska snakes. We sometimes uncovered bull snakes while moving old bales or haystacks on the farm. I'd catch them to give Gordie a closer look. He never saw the humor in it.

We followed the winding river northwest, sometimes crisscrossing slowly, sometimes galloping the horses full-tilt upstream, creating rain and thunder in the sunshine. We were friends under the deep blue Nebraska sky. And in the narrow wilderness of the Elkhorn we were three cowboys of the unexplored West. Partners.

My manhood was being shaped—not by the cowboy fiction of my ideals alone, but by that real land and that real people, wonderfully flawed though they were. I would never be closer to belonging as a son of the Elkhorn.

Meadowlarks cheered us along from their fence posts. Killdeers swooped around us with their shrill alarms, landing on the beaches to dash barefoot across the hard sand. As we came around a bend in the river, several great blue herons rose from a wet sandbar and floated quietly away, following the river into the distance, then rising gracefully into a high stand of cottonwoods.

We rode for several miles—under the bridge on the Summerland Road, over sandbars, around islands, and beyond the forks of the river. At the westward bend just past the sand cliffs known as Yellow Banks, we turned into a narrow canal that carried runoff from the gravel pit on the hill. I was about to be initiated into the academy of hard riding.

We intended to follow the canal only a short distance, then strike out for higher ground to get our bearings and head back to the farm. The hard riding started abruptly fifty yards from the river, but it didn't get us much further than that. All three of us and the three horses beneath us were suddenly engulfed in a pit of quicksand—a hint of reality in the romantic adventure I was planning for my life. It was rodeo at its worst, even though we stuck it out far beyond the eight-second limit.

- VIII -
Parting in New York

Ralph Shrader was a jeans and boots man. I don't know why. But I do know that as a young boy, I saw him as a farm cowboy. He was my Randolph Scott of the Elkhorn, and at times I even lost track of which face was which in my mind. The Lord created Ralph Shrader to ride a horse. So maybe it was not his nature to wear hook-laced high-tops and overalls.

His brother-in-law Wilbur Bennett was an overalls and high-tops man, a stay-at-home Nebraska dirt farmer with two sons and a daughter, a penchant for borrowing, and a seasoned straw hat. Harold, the older of the Bennett boys, was taller and more sinewy than either his dad or his brother, Roger. He was always "Coon" instead of Harold. Roger was husky and strong. His big arms stretched the sleeves of his white T-shirts.

The Bennett farm was on the north side of the road just a quarter mile west of the little schoolhouse next to Grandma Shrader's. The white two-gabled house was set back from the road, hidden on three sides by wide woods which bordered the road and extended north past the farm buildings and into the section toward the "black forest," a heavy stand of large conifers teeming with wildlife. The twin front doors opened south onto a wide verandah. But the doors of common entry opened to the east onto a side porch and into the barnyard. More aged trees towered over the barn and the assorted coops, pens, sheds, and machines, each with its own visible history of hard labor.

Beyond them to the east, the ground sloped under fences and down into the hog lot.

I was five when I first explored the alluring world of the Bennett farm. To a child it was a land of unlimited adventure and mystery. And even the more frightening features of its ramshackle variety—the dark storm cellar, the whispering woods, the scampering critters and great beasts—contributed somehow to an overall air of security, for this was a place of life. It had always been and would forever be. It was home, family, love, prayer, and people working shoulder-to-shoulder. People of hope.

It was also Luella's robust Sunday dinners, which the preacher's family was frequently invited to share. I remember the bustling of mothers and daughters in the kitchen, the wooden slap of the screen door on the east porch, and the jingle of the door hook. I can still see the piano in the living room and on it the framed pictures of Coon and Roger in military uniform. I saw strength and achievement all around me, and I tasted it in heaps of fried chicken.

The men in the pictures occasionally crossed the early stage of my life in person. I stared at them with awe, wondering how I could someday be a man. But I never really knew them.

Roger Bennett died of a heart attack at fifty-nine. I never would have dreamed it. When Belva told me about his death, the someday of being a man had long since arrived in my own life. And the first thing I remembered was the summer of 1964.

In June of that year, I finished high school in California where my dad had accepted a call to pastor a church. By early July, I was eastbound with a high school buddy named Ken. My fall destination was a college in Iowa, but first we made our way from Los Angeles to New York in search of romance and adventure—and the World's Fair if we could fit it in.

I said good-bye to the romance segment of our odyssey early on. Her name was Brigitta, a foreign exchange student and my current eternal flame from high school in California. She had been touring the United States by bus with other foreign students and was scheduled to arrive in New York early in July and return to Austria on a ship called *The Seven Seas*. Ken and I checked into a grungy hotel on Thirty-fourth Street, not knowing the exact date of the ship's departure.

In the hotel lobby I picked up a *Times* and checked the shipping schedules. *The Seven Seas* was leaving that evening, of all things. And Briggie knew nothing of my chase across the continent. In spite of the oppressively muggy weather, I dressed in coat and tie and found my way to the designated pier in lower west Manhattan. I was at the gang plank when buses of students began arriving from points west.

There she was, shocked at first, then telling me that she figured I'd do something like this. My grand scheme was coming together exactly as planned. And it continued that way for another twenty minutes or so.

We boarded the ship as I prepared to unveil my plans for the next phase of our courtship. She preempted me with the unveiling of hers. She would marry her Austrian fiancé after all, and we must not write any more letters. That was the last time I saw her. I walked away in the dark with one of the bigger of my broken hearts. In the subway tunnel I sat crying on a hard bench, wanting to jump in front of the next train and knowing I wouldn't. In my pocket was the thick love letter she had written on the bus trip and mailed to me in California. She had obviously not expected to be held accountable for it so soon.

Alone in the Big Apple with our intellectual curiosities still intact, Ken and I did find adventure—amid varying degrees of danger. It was the summer of the

Harlem race riots, and outsiders were being advised to stay away. So we determined to enter the war zone only long enough to escape and tell. In the middle of one night, we hit the subway near the hotel and headed north to the latitude we figured would be Harlem.

Our figuring was accurate, after a fashion—an unexpectedly welcome fashion. We got off the subway and emerged on the sleeping campus of Columbia University—a quiet sanctuary from the perils we had imagined. Beyond the university's east wall was Harlem. There was a long concrete stairway leading down into a narrow green strip called Morningside Park. We stood at the threshold, squinting down through the trees to the deserted street at the other edge of the park. Isn't this good enough? I wondered. Haven't we proven ourselves? No, we agreed. We haven't set foot in Harlem, not really.

With rubbery knees we crept down the dark steps. That was enough for me. I waited at the bottom, my heart beating hard enough to propel me back to the top if necessary at the first snap of a twig. Ken, for my amusement I believe, decided to pull a John Wayne—even though he was dressed in tight Continental clothes and a stingy-brim hat. Off he went east through the darkness of the trees to the far edge of the park. He stood on the curb, hesitated, then strode across the street and stood briefly under a street light.

That was all I could take. I sprinted up the steps to prepare either for Ken's return or Ken's demise. It was high adventure—the very kind of adventure we had crossed the country to find. And there was more in the ensuing days.

Although we emerged still physically sound, our lost-in-New York odyssey took its toll on our temperaments. We parted ways dramatically one afternoon, walking off through separate terminal gates at the southern tip of Manhattan. Ken boarded a train bound for a graveyard jazz concert in the Bowery, and I didn't see him again until the end of December in Los Angeles.

I had come across the country to regain Brigitta, with a hope for the future that was only a thinly disguised longing for the past. Despite our emotional pledges, I had already lost her in California, and I knew it. Brigitta was gone; Ken was gone. I was no longer a confused ten-year-old looking for Gordie in the back seat of Ralph's Ford at Ewing station.

With a heavy load of emotional souvenirs, I boarded the Staten Island Ferry and gazed out across the water, west, as it cruised into the harbor. In my mind the sparkling wake of the boat was dissolving into the present, and I willfully resisted. From the Statue of Liberty, I could see the Elkhorn.

By late July, I was actually there, arriving in Nebraska by bus to impose myself upon the Shraders for the rest of the summer. It was a year of profound changes.

- IX -
Sixty-Four

My ties to the past, to the Nebraska childhood which I had never fully surrendered, were tugging at me in new ways. From my melancholy perspective, however, Gordie's more substantial ties seemed to be unraveling that summer. Clayton Hoke and I watched from the sidelines as he danced the nights away in park pavilions and Legion halls, his hair dangling over his forehead, his short sleeves rolled high on his lanky arms, and his shirt unbuttoned down past the bulging pack of Winstons. He was devil-may-care, gone wild. Or so we concluded in our timid incredulity.

For the usually unruffled Clayton, it was all rather amusing. For me, it was disconcerting. Gordie was no longer my bespectacled little friend on a big horse in a world extending not much beyond Uncle Wilbur's place. And I had a dismal record of letting go.

Clayton became my reassuring link to both past and future—a future in which Gordie would come to his senses and again be eight years old and "the best pal in the world." More than that, Clayton became the friend whom, since childhood, I had only imagined him to be. During my father's pastorate in Ewing, Clayton Hoke was the mystery boy I never knew— two years older than I and a Methodist. The barriers were high.

Whenever Gordie talked about his friendship with Clayton Hoke, I was rapt with envy. Hokes and Shraders were neighbors on opposite sides of the same section. Their family histories were woven together into sturdy cloth. Like their fathers, Gordie and Clayton attended the one-room country school beside Grandma Shrader's grove. And the accounts of Clayton's speed on Smokey the pony rivaled the heroics of the Friday night movieshows at the Eldorado.

Long after our family had left Nebraska, I mused over a day in 1954 when I went with my dad to call on a Presbyterian farmer up the road from Dewitt Hoke's. Clayton was sitting on the steps of the verandah when we drove by his house on our way home. We waved at each other, and I felt I had met someone famous.

Our next personal contact didn't come until that summer of 1961 when we rode horseback side-by-side and went into the quicksand together. The camaraderie was as fulfilling as our great adventure on the river.

Now it was 1964, and we were swept together in the wake of Gordie's rapid nocturnal flight through the valley. After the summer dances, Clayton would spur his '62 Impala through the darkness of Highway 275 towards Ewing with Chad and Jeremy lamenting "Yesterday's Gone" from the speaker in the empty back seat. We'd gaze out at haystacks dancing by the moon, and always we'd talk about Gordie.

The recent tragedy of Brigitta soon became the opening chapters of the book of Marilyn, Gordie's cousin on a farm a mile east and a mile south of Ralph's. Although the transition was hasty, I didn't really consider myself fickle or emotionally immature. I was too emotionally immature to consider anything of the sort.

Marilyn was a strong but comely farm girl in a petite frame, cheery and wide-eyed, with a husky giggle, blonde curls, and cat's-eye glasses. She accepted my overtures with some enthusiasm, in large part, I believe, because I was the man from California. In the upper

Elkhorn Valley at the time, that distinction was tinted by some of the flair and mystery of movie stars. The image was as hollow as soil pipe, but enjoying its immediate benefits was much easier than accomplishing something worthy of esteem.

My spirits soared with infatuation as I whistled and sang my way through a series of summer jobs—tossing bales; helping to gut an old store on Main Street in Ewing; painting farm buildings for Eddie Shrader, Gordie's bachelor uncle. "We'll Sing in the Sunshine" was one of the hits that summer, and even Nubbins seemed more spirited as I belted it out from his sweaty bare back.

In August, Marilyn started business school in Norfolk. When her first love letter arrived from Norfolk, I read it aloud to Gordie, and we hollered with slack-jawed exhilaration at every line. The door of her heart was wide open, she said, and Gordie and I responded by bouncing off the walls of his bedroom.

The delusion of my new romantic commitment remained strong—until I abandoned it and sweet Marilyn a year and half later as summarily as Brigitta had abandoned me. She found and married someone else within two months.

My emotional nexus with the wider human drama of the obscure upper Elkhorn, however, lay unweakened in a deeper part of my maturity. My childhood Ewing had been a world with close, protected borders and a river flowing through it. Now before me the valley was becoming the world as it is everywhere—with the flow of life not wandering along but charging toward eternity like the muddy waters of the Elkhorn in late spring.

In the summer of 1964, Gordie and I were more concerned about the style of our jeans than about the realities of time and eternity. During a morning of

stacking Ralph's hay on a piece of virgin prairie not far
from Marilyn's place, we sat together on the cabling
rack at break time, observing the older of the men in
their loose fitting hammer-loop work jeans and overalls. They seemed oblivious to the social demands of
fashion. We vowed we'd never be like them, never
wear anything but Levis. We didn't entertain even the
possibility of being anything but skinny and seventeen.

Husky Roger Bennett stood beside the rear wheel of
a tractor about twenty yards away, talking with Gordie's
Uncle Wayne Shrader, nicknamed Judge. There was a
small clink from Roger's Zippo lighter, then a larger
clank as he snapped it shut. The smoke from his cigarette mingled with the aroma of the new hay. It smelled
like toast as it passed us, drifting north. I could see the
bulge of the red and white cigarette pack under the
sleeve of his T-shirt. He was the kind of man I wanted
to be, although I knew my sleeve would never fit my
arm tight enough to hold a pack of cigarettes.

Wilbur Bennett sat slouching on the steel seat of the
old International H with the faded red paint, grinning
through the gaps in his brown teeth and offering occasional commentary in decidedly nasal tones. The labor
exchange was an established institution—more than
that—a cherished institution in the Elkhorn Valley. The
seasons came and went; the years came and went.
Wilbur was in no hurry. Ralph and the other Shraders
would be in the Bennett hayfields soon enough. And
like the Bennett grain fields come fall, they would yield
their harvest to Ralph Shrader's machinery. For Wilbur,
the borrower, never saw the sense in buying his own
equipment when Ralph's was so near at hand.

Ralph's view of the arrangement was made obvious
not by word but by deed. He would have given Wilbur
his last penny had he asked for it.

Behind the tractor rose the wooden stacker,

polished slick by decades of falling hay. Ralph gimped around it on his plastic leg, checking the cable and figuring how long it would take to finish the field.

After break, Gordie and I climbed back up the slippery timbers and waited on top of the hay to shape the growing stack with our pitchforks. From our perch we could see the panorama of the rolling field as several open tractors bounced helter-skelter across the stubble like dancers in a Copland ballet, pulling their wide hay rakes. We could hear the springs screeching heavily as the arched tines were raised and lowered to gather the cut hay into windrows. Ralph on the red Super M-TA was sweeping up the long riffles with his front fork loader and piling the fresh hay on the wooden tines of the stacker.

There was sunshine and health and the joy of working together on God's good field. It was the joy of life, and it was in our eyes as we glanced at one another through our sweat. There was a purpose to it all, a calling as we prepared for the Nebraska winter. And God was preparing us for cold days ahead.

Like his son Roger, Wilbur no longer works that piece of virgin prairie. He is long dead and the ancient grasses long plowed under. Gordie has removed most of the shelter belt at the south end of the field to make way for the irrigation towers that now roll through his high corn. The diesel-powered pivot stands on a hillock in the center of the field of forgotten virginity, where Roger Bennett once stood smoking beside his tractor, joking with Judge and talking of the future, while two miles away to the west Luella was putting the chicken on to fry.

Some people still remember robust Luella and her ready smile and her music. But not many. Not many people remember the alluring world of the Bennett farm at all—with its unlimited adventure and mystery. A bulldozer has built an abrupt hill on the south side of the old farmhouse and one on the north. In summer, an irrigation tower rolls up and over each hill so that the long pivot arm clears the roof. The whispering woods, the scampering critters, the great beasts, the ramshackle barns and sheds—all are gone now. Only the rotting house remains by request of a nostalgic Bennett offspring who lives in another state. Soon it will be gone too, for no one will remember its story or even care.

I stand on the porch looking east across an open draw lined with perfect rows of corn. Irrigation water is raining down, pouring off the roof and in some places dripping through it. And in my sorrow I understand the hope of those strong people. It did not rest in this piece of sandy Nebraska soil, this place of life which now is one of Gordon Shrader's many cornfields. For life is everlasting, and the Bennetts bear their crosses no more. They are not this once strong house that now stands small and alone in a field.

- X -
The Graves
of Frenchtown

The irrigated shell of the Bennett house is not alone in its indignity. Hundreds of forsaken farm and ranch houses stare empty-eyed from the groves and fields of the American roadside. Automobiles speed past them, and the people in the automobiles either take no notice or they fancy quaint little paintings that might match their wallpaper.

Few, if any, remember the fathers and mothers and sons and daughters who once came home to those houses. They do not remember the true stories that would never end—until they did. They do not see in those still-life landscapes the calamity of their own mortality. The earth, like time itself, is suspended from eternity by a thread of tow.

The old, the new—they are twigs of the same tree swallowed by the river. Both are meaningless, a striving after wind.

A mile east of the Hoke farm stands a gravestone shaped like a squared gatepost. It is the only stone in a small plot enclosed by an ornate steel fence. Several irises still grow beside it in the tall weeds. The foremost inscription is "Shrader," and the names "Elsie" and "George" appear on either side—Gordie's great-grandfather Anthony Shrader's children, who died as children, "At Rest" more than a hundred years as I write.

"This lovely flower to us was given to bud on earth

59

to bloom in heaven." The engraved script is almost imperceptible on the weathered stone. "O teach us your will to obey. He gave and he taketh away and pleased be the name of the Lord."

The memories of Elsie and George are less revered even than their obscure grave, for only one or two people know they existed. There are no memories. But that's also true of their brother Albert, who survived the frontier and lived to be Gordie's grandfather. Perhaps as you read this some years from now, the same will be true of Ralph Shrader and Gordon Shrader.

"When their spirit departs," said David the king, "they return to the ground; on that very day their plans come to nothing."

A wider cemetery once surrounded the little fenced Shrader plot, and more than a century ago, the small Elkhorn Valley Presbyterian Church stood nearby. There is no sign of such a church ever existing there in the place that was called Frenchtown Township, for the Frenchtown faithful migrated to the Ewing Presbyterian Church in the late 1880s, and the abandoned building was eventually razed.

Weeds and neglect have consumed whatever there was of the old cemetery. Another gravestone, inscribed "Died Trusting in Jesus," lies toppled under a cedar thicket. There is nothing left behind to trust in. Neither remaining stone can be reached without chopping a path through a wild plum thicket near the quiet dirt road. The only visitors now are coyotes and the deer which make beds in the uncut grasses. Remnants of a cemetery were there when I was a small boy. Every year, a few of the Ewing church families joined us in burning off the weeds. No one has done even that for decades.

The same stillness that consumed the lost gravestones of the old Presbyterian cemetery has swallowed the hollow houses of the abandoned farms beside America's sterile interstates, along its dusty backroads, in countless damp groves and overgrown coves, on treeless prairie hills far from modern commerce. Most of the names have disappeared, and there's no one left to lay flowers or even know where to lay them.

"There is no remembrance of men of old," says the Teacher, son of David. "And even those who are yet to come will not be remembered by those who follow." Time is like the Elkhorn, bearing all its sons away. That's Gordie, and Clayton, and I. We fly forgotten as a dream.

But never think that the names in this book—Shrader, Hoke, Biddlecome, Gunter, Hohman, Bennett—are nothing more than grave rubbings. For they live on after we forget, embracing the eternal wisdom of Solomon without confusion and without sorrow. Their hope has been realized, and it was not in things under the sun. Those crumbled like memory and granite.

- XI -
Vanishing People

Digging into the stillness of the upper Elkhorn pioneers is like burning off the weeds of an abandoned cemetery. The names appear, and then, for a sobering moment, I see the people themselves, alive with their descendants on their laps, telling them the old stories that are suddenly new.

Shelbyville, Illinois, 1862. Whenever William Hoke saw blue coats in the distance, he ran to hide until they had marched by. It wasn't a matter of dodging service for the Union, for he was a child of six. It was a matter of his being unprepared to see his sheltered world opened up much beyond the banks of the nearby Kaskaskia River. And he was struck with a certain terror to think that it could be ripped open by sword.

With transparent joy, Dewitt Hoke shares such faraway accounts of his father's life. His recollections measure almost a century and a half, for the days of both William Hoke and his son were destined to be "long upon the earth."

Six-year-old William's Pennsylvania Dutch family had only recently come to Illinois by wagon train from Lebanon, Pennsylvania. Now there were dark clouds over the promised land. The soldiers were marching south to war. And somewhere among them were men whose lives would someday merge with the life of this incredulous little boy. For after the war, their family trees would grow tall as Nebraska cottonwoods by the Elkhorn River, branches intertwining.

Thirty-nine-year-old Anthony Shrader was heading south with Company 1 of the Second Illinois Artillery. It was hard service. His father, John, was a Virginian, the son of a 1776 Hessian immigrant, and Anthony himself was a Virginian come west from Amherst seeking land, not war. He had not known he was coming north as well—politically. And he didn't know, even as he listened day after day to the caissons creaking along, the horrors he would survive at Chickamauga and Chattanooga.

Calvin Gunter, a farm boy of twenty from across the Mississippi at Keosauqua, Iowa, was marching south too with a tintype of Ruth Teague in the pocket of his blue coat. He would also survive the war to be mustered out of service in 1865 with $52.42 in severance pay and his sweetheart's picture still in his pocket.

Across continents, over fields of battle, along trails of pioneers, and into the remote wilderness of the Elkhorn, the winds of God blew the ancestral seeds of my lifelong friends, Gordon Shrader and Clayton Hoke. In the soil beside the river, those seeds germinated, sent down roots, and sprouted into decades of sturdy stalks and delicate blossoms. Together they turned the fallow prairie into fields of color flourishing in the Nebraska sun.

After the terrible war, Anthony Shrader took twenty-five-year-old Mary Lake to be his wife. In 1883, fifteen years later, they left Livingston, Illinois, for the Elkhorn Valley. And someday in another century, a thin little boy in wire-rimmed glasses would carry his name up a sandy Nebraska road on a black horse named Nubbins with William Hoke's grandson at his side.

Clayton Hoke's great-grandfather Calvin Gunter returned from the war to marry his sweetheart in Iowa. After six years of marriage, he and Ruth drove their ox team west. There in a dugout beside the Elkhorn they survived together on wild game and corn meal, far from war.

Then William Hoke came to the Elkhorn Valley, no longer a child running to hide from the adversities of the real world. With bold spirit and his bride, Lettie, at his side, he had met the challenge to "go west, young man, go west," leaving the good soil of "Ioway" to seek cheaper land and the costly dignity of a pioneer.

In May, 1884, he carried Lettie over the threshold of their first house, two miles east of the river. Ewing's articles of incorporation were seventeen days old.

Under the terms of the 1878 Timber Culture Act, he signed an agreement to plant ash, cottonwood, and box elder trees alongside his own roots in the sandy soil of "The Tree Planting State," thus relieving the tax burden on that part of his quarter-section homestead. Two years later, in 1886, he bought another full quarter beside his homestead. It was the beginning of the Hoke farm and a legacy that lives today, more than a century later.

In 1897, William erected a monument on a hill overlooking the Elkhorn. "None knew thee but to love thee," the inscription read. "None named thee but to praise." Lettie was forever thirty-nine. Together they had survived the prairie fires and floods of frontier Nebraska. They had endured the Great Blizzard of '88, when half of the livestock in Holt County perished. They had endured the Great Drouth of '90, when all the crops failed. But the grass of their own humanity withered and the flowers fell. Together they could not find shelter from the storm of time.

The Ewing Cemetery has grown around Lettie's solitary grave for a hundred years, and her husband lies nearby with another wife.

In February of 1900, three years after Lettie's death, William gave the hand of their daughter, Elsie, to the twenty-eight-year-old son of Calvin and Ruth Gunter. James Gunter and Elsie eventually honored her father with thirteen grandchildren born with Lettie's blood flowing in their veins.

William himself remained alone for only a few years. His daughter's marriage created closer ties with the Gunter family and much closer ties with his son-in-law's oldest sister, Jane, called Jennie. She became his second wife.

Jennie gave William a son, Dewitt, in October of 1905. William was forty-nine. He had come half a century from the days of the blue coats marching through Shelbyville on the Kaskaskia River in central "Illinoise." He would live nearly half a century more on the homestead he and Lettie had first carved out of the Nebraska prairie.

These people of an earlier century—William Hoke, Anthony Shrader, Calvin Gunter—met the seasons with the hope of glory. Their callused hands were too full to embrace the idle gods of Modernism that were distilling cynicism and gin in the industrialized east. "God seemed to goad all of them to their utmost capacity, mental and physical," remembered Antelope County pioneer E.P. McCormick in his 1909 memoir.

In their harsh and simple world, they accepted the reality of truth and beauty as naturally as they did the reality of the soil and the river. It was good that they didn't know how soon and how quietly they would vanish from the earth.

- XII -
Schoolhouse Snapshot

In the year of Dewitt Hoke's birth, old Anthony Shrader's son Albert was married in the white Presbyterian church in Ewing. He and May Shrader moved into a little house across the section north of Hokes'. Their first son was born two years later.

On a sunny day less than a decade after that, as the faraway world was preparing for "The War To End All Wars," Dewitt Hoke and Ralph Shrader sat together in a one-room schoolhouse on the edge of the willow grove west of the Shrader house, safe within the long-insulated Elkhorn Valley. Ralph's first monthly report card for the year was in the flap pocket of his overalls.

Attitude to School Work: "wastes time." Recitation: "comes poorly prepared." Conduct: "inclined to mischief." The critical issues of life were recitation and the approaching corn harvest. The grimmest threat during the school year was not the bayonet or the bullet, but the official warning engraved on Antelope County report cards: "The young man who smokes cigarettes need not worry about his future. He has none." Europe was a faraway fantasy, farther even than Omaha or Lincoln.

After school, the two boys galloped their horses together up and down the road, then finally trotted west to the corner. There Dewitt turned into the narrow, grassy road which led to his home a mile south. Ralph, his report card pressing heavily against his chest, turned back east for May's cookies and milk before heading to the barn for chores.

- XIII -
Invaders

The old verandah has been gone from the south side
of the Hoke house for years. The elms that grew beside the lane are gone too. Dewitt is still here, William Hoke's son, looking through the windows of his
trailer house at nearly a hundred years of this place
and remembering Florence, his wife. He has seen
more than trees and porches come and go.

It will soon be a century since he sat on Calvin
Gunter's lap, combing his curious little fingers through
his grandpa's long white beard and hearing his stories of
the frontier while Uncle Dewitt Gunter played his
fiddle in the dining room.

Grandpa Gunter had seen the eerie red glow of
approaching prairie fires against the distant fall sky.
He told about taking refuge in the Elkhorn to escape
them—the firestorm of '78 being particularly memo-
rable.

He recalled the Easter Storm of 1873, the dreadful
three-day blizzard that cut down livestock and wildlife
alike, driving so much snow into the Elkhorn that both
the river and its high banks disappeared under a white
plain. After the storm, he had walked south from his log
cabin and crossed the snow-packed river without any
visible sign of where it lay.

He told also of the Sioux raiders who had come
into the upper Elkhorn Valley in February of 1870,
less than three months before the arrival of James
Ewing on the Elkhorn County frontier. They invaded
the homes of several settlers in western Antelope
County and stole their horses.

On the evening of the twenty-seventh, ten painted braves barged into Martin Freeman's cabin located a couple of miles south of what became Ralph Shrader's place a century later. They wore feathers in their hair and were armed with bows and arrows and guns. Martin had gone east looking for winter work, leaving his younger brother to care for his wife and baby.

During the five-hour ordeal, Mrs. Freeman briefly escaped in hopes of fetching help from other settlers. Two of the braves ran her down and threatened to take her "papoose" unless she returned home. After eating and resting, they left the "heap good squaw" without inflicting any physical harm.

The next day, they shot up Louis Patras's cabin two miles down river. After killing chickens and shooting a cow, they trotted off toward the Elkhorn, leaving the family terrified but otherwise unharmed. That night, they stole ten horses—one apiece—from six homesteads. The animals were later recovered by soldiers from north of the Niobrara at Fort Randall.

In November, another hostile band of Sioux struck again. Eleven braves ransacked the new cabin of Robert Horne, stealing what they could carry and ravaging everything else. This time, a company of fourteen settlers took out after them, following their faint trail upstream into vast Elkhorn County.

Just beyond James Ewing's claim, where the town of Ewing is now located, the pursuers sent a couple of their men across the Elkhorn to search the south bank for tracks as they paralleled the main party up the valley. About five hours later, shortly before nightfall, they encountered the raiders near the present site of O'Neill. Their challenge was quickly met with gunfire followed by a continuous barrage of arrows. The settlers packed superior arms, including a Spencer and a Sharps, and the battle was brief. The Indian band was driven off with its chief severely wounded. Several of the settlers returned home perforated with flint, but no one was killed.

Several months after the bloody encounter, two of the original posse rode back up river to survey the field of battle. Much to their wonder, the Sioux had returned before them and ceremoniously broken every spent arrow, leaving it in two pieces where it had fallen in the battle.

The settlers were agitated enough by the whole affair to organize a militia called the Elkhorn Guards. But it never saw action. Except for one other horse-stealing incursion into Frenchtown in the spring of 1874, hostile Sioux never again caused trouble in Antelope County.

Although Grandpa Gunter recalled with some drama those timorous early years of the Sioux insurgency, he became more animated when he came to describe the hordes of winged invaders that came annually in the first years of settlement. The grasshopper plague had been the most discouraging thing ever to strike the early settlers.

It began in 1867 as a random nuisance. But by 1872, the grasshoppers were coming by the billions with the sound of storm, devouring crops in the places where they descended. Heavy grasshopper clouds darkened the sky, then like sparkling snow fell to the fields with an eerie silver-winged grace. Men forced to walk through them had to tie shut the cuffs of their pants to keep their bare legs from being covered like the cornstalks. And they had to keep their mouths shut.

The voracious invaders stripped the leaves from the trees (box elders were exempt) and the bark from their smaller branches. They destroyed garments on clotheslines and even harness leather and the latigo on saddles.

Women covered their favorite plants with carpets,

and the grasshoppers destroyed both the carpets and the plants. Chickens ate so many grasshoppers that for a while their meat was unfit for human consumption. Even the trains stopped running because the smothering masses of grasshoppers made the tracks too slippery.

The plague continued seasonally for ten years until it was itself terminally plagued by red mites that bore through the chitinous armor of the invading hordes. After 1877, the suffocating swarms never came again.

The grasshoppers were so bad in 1874 that the weight of them broke branches off the trees. Great grasshopper clouds dimmed the sun for hours at a time—sometimes whole days—as they drifted southeastward. The six-year Indian Wars began that year. But neither the fear of attack in the conflict between the U.S. Cavalry and the Sioux nor even the widespread bloodletting among tribes was a match for the plague from the western skies. It was remembered as "The Grasshopper Year."

That fall, Calvin Gunter watched the ill-fated Gordon Party rumble through the valley with six covered wagons, blazing what was to be the Black Hills Trail on the ridge above his dugout.

John Gordon had been hired by unscrupulous investors to lead a wagon train of prospectors and their families from Iowa to the gold-rich Black Hills of South Dakota. The U.S. government had made a treaty with the Sioux in 1868, guaranteeing their exclusive ownership of the Black Hills. For whites, even entering the Black Hills was strictly forbidden by federal law.

The twenty-six scofflaw pioneers reached the Black Hills in December, after a seventy-day journey. They began panning and soon found gold. The venture seemed an immediate success.

The ease of violating the treaty, however, made the intruders precariously heady. In February of 1875, they sent Gordon and one of the other squatters back east to Sioux City for supplies and reinforcements. In March, a larger company—174 souls—struck out with twenty-nine wagons loaded with families and their possessions. The train followed the Elkhorn west into the Sand Hills and eventually linked up with the Niobrara in western Nebraska.

On May 25, the great illegal enterprise was intercepted by U.S. Cavalry troops from Fort Randall. They arrested the would-be miners and burned the entire wagon train—lock, stock, and furniture.

The town subsequently established on the site of charred wood and shattered dreams bore the name Gordon.

Grandpa's stories seemed ancient even then, nearly a century ago, as new stories were being made. There I see Dewitt, a boy of five excitedly running around on the foundation of the new house being built by his father, William—a house with a front porch for Jennie. It is an early summer day in 1910, after the seed corn is in the ground. Lettie's homesteading house is only twenty-six years old, but Lettie is gone and it is time now to give Jennie a house on high ground—a "proper" house just for her, far from the Gunter dugout where she learned to sweep on a dirt floor.

Looking again, I see Dewitt today, a small, strong man true to his Gunter blood, smaller now in old age. But the mirth in his eyes is still large, his easy chuckle still frequent, and his handshake still firm. "Back in those days, it was a pretty good life."

Clayton's family lives in Jennie's proper house now—and has lived there since Florence died, years ago. Clayton's son, Aaron, represents the fourth Hoke generation to work the soil of the old homestead.

From this place the sandy road runs a mile west and ends at the crossroad. It used to extend further west where, long ago, William Hoke and his neighbors cut a more-or-less direct route all the way to town. For a mile beyond the intersection, remnants of the old road can still be found shriveled in old age and succumbing to a tangle of wild plum, locust, and poison ivy. On either side are the gnarled descendants of two five-row shelter belts. Further west there is no trace of road at all anymore, just jungle and swamp secluding the river beyond.

Here, long ago, young Dewitt rode his horse to the Elkhorn where he'd cross the bridge and wind on through the woods to cross a swamp bridge and curve into Ewing for high school. He loved that colubrine old road in a way he loved no other part of the valley. "Used to be, there was no road in the county like it."

Even in his ninetieth year, he remembered the colors, "It was beautiful in the spring and beautiful in the fall." In the winter, Ralph Shrader often turned his horse south from Bennetts' corner to meet Dewitt and ride with him through the shelter of the thick woods. "It was nice in the winter when the wind was blowing. At one time, we counted the turns. There were around fifteen. It was kinda crooked."

There were many quiet afternoons when Dewitt, alone, dismounted at the river bridge and tossed sticks into the clear water. They bobbed away southeast, and he wondered into what kind of a world they would go. He thought perhaps someday he would follow. But he never did.

He had been on the Elkhorn many times, but never, never to float away. As a child he had played for hours on the riverbanks upstream at Grandpa Gunter's place. In the winters, he had ice skated there on the river with his friends, scanning the wooded banks for treasures. For he knew the story of old man Ford who had been buried somewhere south of Grandpa's house in the earliest days of Ewing's pioneers.

A spring flood, years before Dewitt was born, had pushed the river into new channels, washing away the grave and even threatening the Gunter house far back through the woods. When winter came, children skating on the river had found Ford's skull and some of his bones. The skull was taken to town and hung on a nail in the office of the *Ewing Advocate*, where it was still hanging in Dewitt's youth.

There were occasions in Dewitt's high school years when the river "was pretty ferocious," and the spring floods kept him and his horse far from the bridge for weeks at a time. He had to tie his horse upstream at Gunters', then board a flatboat operated by two sometimes-ferrymen. After crossing a quarter mile of water near the county road bridge, he'd walk on south into town for school.

In late fall, the river was low and calm. But there was never much time to linger on the east bridge after school. The corn picking in those days was done by hand, and Dewitt's young hands were needed at home. In the field, he walked quickly and picked ears as he went, being careful to stay near the front of the corn wagon. Getting struck by a heavy ear tossed by another picker was reminder enough to stay in position.

It was not uncommon to pick corn until sundown, come in to milk the cows before eating supper, then, after supper, unload the corn in the dark with scoop shovels. Even in his early boyhood, Dewitt had been known to scoop as much or more than a man could.

When work was done, he finally headed to the house, carrying a load of last year's cobs to burn in the stove. Then, weary, he fell asleep reading his assignments by the light of the acetylene lamp.

For several winters, he helped Uncle Jim with the

Gunters' ice business, cutting 300-pound blocks from Pickerel Lake to store in the large ice house or deliver directly to town. The "lake" was actually no more than a narrow river bayou beside the county road, but big enough for working a team of horses on the ice. They pulled a plow beam set with vertical knives, then the men sawed the ice blocks free with a horizontal saw.

Gunters' ice wagon plied the streets of Ewing making a delivery wherever a large "ICE" card was displayed in a window. The wagon usually had a following of children waiting to suck on the ice chips created when a block had to be custom cut for someone's ice box.

Each Saturday afternoon, Dewitt carted home a small block of ice for making the treat of the week. With plenty of homegrown milk and cream and eggs, there "wasn't hardly a Sunday but what we had ice cream."

- XIV -
The Old Bottom Road

When I was a boy in the Ewing of the early fifties, there was still more than a remnant of that old bridge west of Hokes'. I rode my hand-me-down brown bike to the county road stop sign at the east end of Main Street. (It was actually Nebraska Street, but there were no street signs in those days, and everyone called it "Main Street." Another street at the west end of town actually bore that name, but contrary to the intentions of the early town fathers, it never lived up to it.)

The intersection was one of the few places in town where I dutifully remembered to "look both ways." To the right, the county road led south to the highway; to the left, it led over the steel Elkhorn River bridge and on north between Gunters' and Biddlecomes'.

Squeezing my cane pole to the handlebars, I pedaled straight across and down the narrow old "Bottom Road" east into the dark green woods. It curved north a bit past the shack where an elderly couple named Pollock still lived, then east again to where there were no creatures but ghosts and bullfrogs. Beside the road were green lagoons and old fences with posts made of crooked branches. Most of the board railings were gone from the swamp bridge, and I'd ride across with pounding heart, swerving to avoid the chasms where chunks of bed planking had rotted away.

Although cars still occasionally crossed here on Sunday afternoons, I believed I was one of few adventurers to know these remote wooded reaches. I had no idea that the colubrine trail from here to the river had once been a common route of local commerce. I had no idea that a boy named Dewitt had long before crossed this bridge daily on a horse. I didn't even attribute its existence to human construction. It came to me only from some ancient existence of its own.

Somewhere in the woods west of the rickety river bridge, I laid my bike in the sand and caught grasshoppers for bait. They were plentiful and seemed always to work better than worms. I knew from school that the grasshoppers wouldn't bite. But I never caught one that didn't make me wince with its saw-toothed kicks and tobacco spit.

Nothing ever pulled bluegills and sunfish from the quiet ponds better than my bamboo pole and grasshoppers. I strung my catch on a willow twig and walked my bike back across the bridge to prevent my new cargo from swinging me off balance. Every time I reemerged from that faraway land and into the sunshine of Ewing, it was like coming out of a Friday night movieshow at the Eldorado, where I was Randolph Scott.

Now as I wander through the swampy woods on foot, I can pick up bits and pieces of the old road where the ruts are still deep. The only remaining evidence of the river crossing are the stubs of several bridge pilings standing in the shallow water below the Yellow Banks. The only signs left of that ancient bridge in the swamps are an arch of concrete near the west bank of a lagoon—and these memories. In a few years, those will be gone too.

- XV -
Sarah

Although the old Bottom Road, ever seeking the river, at last doddered alone through the forest and died in the swamps, my lone seeking of the Elkhorn didn't end with my childhood. During my Iowa college years, I returned many times to explore the river's bayous and bars downstream from the Summerland Road south of Shraders'.

The woods were alive with game in all seasons. The high sandy banks were peppered with the tracks of coyotes, deer, raccoons, and sometimes bobcats. The clean level sands along the shallow water held the spidery imprints of herons' feet and the fine parallel ruts of turtles. In the sun lay bleached sticks of various sizes delivered by the river from beaver dams somewhere upstream. The distinct chisel marks of beaver teeth covered their pointed ends.

Several miles upstream, beyond the old Bottom Road, was Biddlecome land where I often sat musing on the banks of the Elkhorn—land largely unchanged since the days of Adam Hohman. Gordie was in Lincoln at the university, and I usually stayed with Shraders during my weekend escapes to Nebraska. But I wandered many days away here on the old Hohman homestead, exploring the green hills and gullies west of the barn and hunting in the woods from there to the river. It was my own paradise, if solitude could be paradise. In late spring, each small pond in the resplendent green meadows was encircled by a wide halo of dandelions. Come summer, the

yellow of the dandelions yielded to sunflowers which
wandered into the woodlands. By fall, the yellow had
crept to the edge of the river in sprays of buttercups.

Adam Hohman was eighteen when he sailed to
America from Germany in 1865. In 1880, he came
west to the Elkhorn River Valley with his wife, Tamar,
and their two daughters. Nellie was seven, and Sarah
was six—girls who in old age would roll their buck-
boards through my life. Adam filed for land and became the first blacksmith for Ford village, soon to be
called Ewing.

The following year, before the railroad tracks had
reached this far up the valley, he drove a team of four
horses twenty miles down river to Neligh and returned
with a wagonload of lumber.

He hired an old carpenter named Bucker to begin
building on his homestead land across the river north of
the village. The house that rose out of the Nebraska
prairie was German straight and American proud with a
high peaked roof and tall windows facing east from the
parlor.

The precise construction of the Hohman farm re-
flected more than a scrupulous German heritage. In the
hard and simple life of the valley, there was attention to
small things as well as large. In 1889, Sarah's final
eighth-grade report card came back from Ewing
School with a recorded cumulative average of 91 1/11.
She had earned it. Accomplishment was measured not
so much in the light of economic return as it was in
light of human dignity.

Nor were the smallest of God's natural blessings
trivialized or taken for granted. Every spring, Nellie and
Sarah climbed the trees by the river to harvest wild
grapes from the high creeping vines. It was the season
for the blessing of green grape pie. Every summer, they
climbed the trees again to harvest ripe grapes for the
blessing of grape jelly.

The valley in those days was also flowing with the milk and honey of sand cherries, choke cherries, wild plums, buffalo berries, and currants. Perhaps that word "flowing," used here in the biblical sense, carries some irony into the present, for much of that wild fruitfulness has somehow flowed off with time.

The domestic harvests were bountiful as well. The girls spent their summers hoeing sunflowers and cockleburs out of the hand-planted corn. In the fall, it yielded thirty-plus bushels per acre. Yearling calves brought one to three dollars each, and, in a strong market, a pound of homemade butter sold for as much as fourteen cents.

One of the most cherished of blessings on the Hohman farm was Sarah herself—hardworking, God-fearing Sarah. Before her graduation from Ewing High in 1893, she expressed her honest view of being human in an essay simply titled "Life."

"In this life," she said, "only we have hope in Christ, or we are of all men most miserable. . . . Youth is the time to prepare for after life, and not wait till death comes to repent. It is generally too late then. . . . We have the promise of the life that now is, and of the life which is to come. . . . Is not the life more than meat, and the body than raiment?"

That same spring, Adam fattened a steer and hauled it all of the hundred miles to Sioux City with a four-horse team. It took him a week. He went shopping after the sale and bought a gold watch for each of his daughters—the kind of watch that hung from a necklace. Although they were a year apart in age, Nellie and Sarah were graduating together. Adam also bought pink cashmere for graduation dresses, five cents per yard. A Ewing seamstress named Mrs. Gilmore came out to the farm to sew the dresses. With love, life is more than fattened steers and the body more than cashmere.

By 1907, Sarah the woman had made the uncommon decision to strike out on her own with horse and wagon—two hundred miles into the western prairie near Mullen. In the wilderness west of the Giant Hill, she staked a claim for homestead land—160 acres. It was a commitment to five years of "proving up," the verifiable continuous residence required to secure the deed.

The Preemption Claim option of entitlement forthwith at $1.25 an acre was not a viable one for most Nebraska homesteaders. Personal hardship was a resource more readily available than cash. And with that resource, Sarah planted herself firmly in her sod ("Nebraska marble") house above the Middle Loup River on the open grassland of the Sand Hills.

Sarah's years on the Mullen homestead proved up to be a personal hardship for her father as well. Oliver Conner had taken his eldest daughter, Nellie, away to start a home up the ridge a half-mile east. But Sarah had taken Sarah away, and Adam longed to have her back. His wife, Tamar, was "poorly," and he needed Sarah's help at home.

In the last months before her required five years was complete, his letters began to flow. Every one included wistful descriptions of the life she was missing at Ewing and references to "when you come home."

"There is lotts of grapes you be hear and fill our jars and Cans Mama had three tups full of grapes on hand that I and Arba pickt."

And later: "That Chicken house is don and Mama says she would Like to moove into it herself." He had built a handsome "stone" chicken house by casting his own blocks in rounded molds. Beside it was his wooden shop where he pumped his large blacksmith's bellows.

"Mama wishes you wher hear to help her Cook She is laying on the Couch a snorring," wrote Adam in June. His letters were frequent.

That summer, 1912, Sarah also began to receive

loving letters of remonstrance from various other members of the family back in Ewing. Her homestead title would be secure by November, and her diligent work had been sorely missed for these five years. Tamar was usually abed and Nellie was aghast at the thought of feeding the haying crews for even one more summer. They wanted her back. The risk of her settling down at Mullen was unnerving.

In July, sister Nellie applied her subtle hand, "Well, Sarah as long as mother is so poorly, we couldn't think of going off & leave her. You must come home as soon as you prove up, for mother is wishing for you every day."

An August letter from her adopted brother, Arba, laid it out in plain English. "Ma says she wished you were home so you could do the work." By late October, however, he had adjusted to the endearing, off-hand approach. "Say, when do you think you'll be home?"

"If you dond get Away from up ther soon you will have a Cold hyhr again," warned her dad that same month.

On November 12, the Department of Interior Land Office at Broken Bow affirmed Sarah's independent endurance—"Testimony fee & commissions in final proof in connection with Homestead, serial no. 03653. Receipt $6.00." It was done. The pressure of her legal obligation was relieved, but the pressure of her family still weighed heavily. She returned to the Elkhorn Valley that same month.

Six years later, she had her covered wagon packed again. A flu epidemic was sweeping up the valley, and she was ready to flee to the Mullen homestead with Lucille and Phyllis, her newly-adopted daughters. She had wanted all along to have her own place, and the time had come to break away for good. No amount of cajoling would draw her back this time.

There was no cajoling. Her relatives had come to

rely more than ever on her diligent work on the farm and the able care she provided for her ailing mother. "You're not going," they said. They untied her milk cows from behind the wagon and unloaded her furniture.

But Tamar was not long for this world beside the Elkhorn River. Adam moved her into town later that year and hired a nurse to care for her. She died in 1919, and Sarah's obligatory fences were cut. Her other brother George's ranching venture in the Sand Hills was bankrupt, and he was moving his family of nine back to the home place. It was time to leave. No one pulled the furniture back off her wagon.

She had dreamed of the Missouri Ozarks ever since reading an ad in some paper. Adam needed to get away, so he agreed to take Arba with him on a train to Missouri and check things out for Sarah. The land agent from Mountain View showed them all the colorful and prosperous places, but not the place he subsequently arranged to sell to Sarah. They brought back exuberant reports. Fanciful Sarah sold the Mullen homestead— dobie, fences, open vistas, and all—and struck out for the Ozarks farm of her dreams with Lucille and Phyllis and her dignified determination in tow. She filled three boxcars with cows, horses, machinery, chickens— everything.

The dream soon slipped away like the hard-earned homestead in the Sand Hills. What awaited her was nothing like the proud German farm she had known beside the Elkhorn. It was, she discovered to her dismay, not a farm in the Nebraska sense of the word. It was stones and timber and stones and stones.

She struggled for three years to provide for her small family and meet the mortgage payments. Neither was successful. Nor was her desperate love for a Missouri gentleman who, ironically, also bore the name Hohman. Names weren't enough to unite them. His heart was no less stony than the Ozark soil.

The unscrupulous land agent pocketed the fruits of her five hard years of Nebraska homesteading. With her remaining possessions in a single boxcar, Sarah returned to Nebraska defeated and broken-hearted, having lost all but her daughters and a man's brown photograph upon which she had written, "My Beloved."

- XVI -
A Heart's-eye View

Sarah Hohman's oldest daughter, Lucille, always had a problem with animals—even after she was Keith Biddlecome's wife. She loved them too much.

She fussed like a mamma with a sick child whenever a cow had to be butchered or loaded into a wagon on sale-barn day. As a young woman, she was frequently seen sitting on a stump out in the pasture by the Elkhorn, surrounded closely by cows lying in the grass and chewing their cud. She drew them together only by crawling through the barbed-wire fence and strolling out past the pond without so much as a "come boss!" or a whistle.

In the midst of her "babies" she sang, for she loved to sing. And she spoke to them one-by-one, for she knew them by name. She cooed over each in turn with hugs and kisses and a bit of rubbing and scratching. This was Lucille, always. She never grew out of herself.

As I spent more and more time at Biddlecomes' in the late sixties, I began sleeping in the loft of their crooked old house—the house that Adam Hohman had built so straight in 1881. Some mornings I walked with Lucille out through the garden and into the pasture. The cows shied at my presence, but it was not enough to hold them in abeyance for long. They crowded around Lucille—grown cows with calves of their own, acting like calves themselves. She purred to each one, massaging and hugging, all the while sweetly admonishing the more jealous of the group to await their turns.

Other farmers, dead serious, told me that Lucille Biddlecome was ruining those cows and didn't understand farming. "Oh," I thought.

Lucille's affectionate proclivities were perfectly acceptable to Keith. But he wasn't fully a farmer. For years, he was on the road, selling. Then he commuted to a job in Norfolk ("Norfork" to people in the valley). Keith Biddlecome came very close to retirement. He also came very close to home one Friday night after driving with Lucille from Norfork in a blizzard. He didn't reach retirement or home either one. He pulled off on the shoulder of the county road at the southeast corner of Ewing, shifted into park, and was dead of a heart attack. When the sheriff's car came along, the headlights of Keith's car were still shining into the whiteness of the storm. Lucille said it was a fine thing to die so easily. The Lord is so good, she said.

The pillaging of the Biddlecome farm—the Hohman heritage—began after that.

Lucille had come to the upper Elkhorn Valley when she was three. That never would have happened had Cecil Drew Dearth, her birth mother, survived the black tongue diphtheria back in Burlington, Iowa, where bewildered physicians had exiled her to die in a hospital storage room at nineteen.

Nor would it have happened had Lucille's father, Henry Aaron Dearth, known how to read when he came with his two little girls to Omaha in 1916, looking for work. The Lord works in mysterious ways. At first, Henry hired babysitters; they proved untrustworthy. He then found reputable care for his daughters at the Child Saving Institute. He signed the papers with his X and went off in hopes of earning enough money to establish a new home for his family. When he returned one day, his little girls were gone. He had affixed his X to an adoption release thinking it was a contract for child care.

The Institute refused to tell him who had taken the girls. And there was little recourse for a poor, uneducated man in those times. It was nearly half a century later when Lucille and her sister saw him again—the only father they had ever known. He had spent decades trying to find them.

The woman who became their new mother in 1916 never married. She was a forty-two-year-old farmer's daughter from Ewing—Sarah Hohman.

Supported by testimonials and affidavits from the elders of the Ewing Presbyterian Church, Sarah had secured licensure from the state adoption service. She eventually made the long trip to Omaha, returning with two little girls to raise on her father's farm beside the Elkhorn River, "with the Bible, old adages, and a stick above the kitchen door," Lucille told me, many years later.

One of those favorite old adages was "God takes care of fools and children." It proved true enough. Another was "Never say I can't." And for eighty-eight years, Sarah almost never did.

Long after the Hohman farm had become the Biddlecome farm, I stood in the doorway of Adam's sagging blacksmith shop awestruck by the treasures it held. Cobwebs and dirt covered and bound together generations of Hohman skeletons. The old bellows stood on end in the far corner. Two crockery jugs sat in the dirt under bedsteads and chairs made from branches. I pulled both jugs out and set them on a straw bale in the yard next to the stone chicken house. One of them, the white one with the round top, had a blue flower painted on it. The other one was plain white. I took one photograph then reinterred them in their mausoleum.

Nothing was for sale on Lucille Biddlecome's place—the heritage of Adam Hohman, her grandfather, and Sarah, her mother. And I understood that. She cherished the farm, the heirlooms, no less than she so softheartedly cherished each of the animals in the field.

While she was working weekdays at the state hospital in Norfolk after Keith died, antique scavengers with long feelers began to crawl out of the swamps of faraway cities and slither into the valley. Eventually, little of value was left on the old farm. The thieves even took things of no use and no meaning to anyone but the poor widow who loved her poor home. But they took more than merchandise; they took the way things had been.

One weekend in this so empty, so quiet house, Keith came back. Lucille longed for him more than ever, longed to hear him come walking into the house again, and from her bed in the dead of night, she did. She wasn't afraid, for she knew it was he coming in through the kitchen. He sat beside her, undressed, and got into bed. "How did you get into the house?" she asked him.

"You left the door unlocked," he said. When she awoke in the morning, she jumped out of bed and ran out to check the door. It was locked.

"A dream comes when there are many cares," the Teacher of wisdom once said. The dream is meaningless, he wrote, for it is soon past and the past is forgotten.

In this once fine white house, Adam Hohman raised his four children. In this house, his daughter Sarah gathered her two adopted daughters under the rafters of Adam and Tamar's stern piety. In this house, Lucille became a woman and a mother and a widow. Three long generations came and went, and no more.

In this house, when I was twenty, I lay upstairs on a summer night in the darkest quiet of Nebraska. Sioux warriors with beaded war clubs rode their ponies past the storm cave below my window, then out through the pasture and on south into the trees by the river. Though the window beside my bed was open, I could not hear their whispering hoofbeats—only the howl of the buffalo wolves.

North of the house several freight wagons rumbled along the low ridge above the barn, each following seven yoke of oxen west to the gold-fevered Black Hills. They were laden with flour and feed from the river mill at Neligh. The bullwhackers cracked thirty-foot whips and all wore pistols, knowing that hostile Sioux had attacked and murdered other wagoners on this route.

Long after they passed, a stagecoach appeared out of the east and rolled across the ridge like a phantom, vanishing into the western darkness behind the freight wagons. Its passengers never knew I was there. They heard only the cicadas rasping and the coyotes yapping beneath the lone cottonwood at the far end of the corral.

In the morning, Lucille cooked up my favorite Biddlecome breakfast: browned potatoes, oven-toasted bread, thick bacon, and eggs fried crisp in the deep grease. She served it all heaped on a white crockery platter like a haystack on a cabling rack. We sat there together—Keith, Lucille, and I—insulated momentarily from the changing currents of our lives. But the old house was whispering words of time in our ears.

On the table, my glass sloped perpendicular to the slope of the kitchen floor—an angle emphasized by the horizon of the milk it held. For in the house's old age, each room had taken on a character and an angle of its own. Even here in the peaceful joy of the Elkhorn Valley, there was no isolation from decay.

After breakfast, I carried my rifle out across the

garden with the black orphan He-She panting expect-
antly at my heel. Lucille's sweet corn was taller than
both of us. In its shadows something on the ground
caught my eye. I bent down and picked up a flint ar-
rowhead lying fully exposed in the sand. He-She
sniffed it briefly in my hand and gave me a knowing
look. It was Sioux.

Beyond the old stone shed, we crawled through
the corral fence and walked together past the windmill and the big cottonwood and through the pasture
gate. A cow path led us into the trees where the dog
assumed its hunting character, padding beside me
with discreet silence, and crouching whenever I
stopped to listen for game. Soon we climbed up from
the woods, past the old Pawnee grave site to the top
of the ridge where Lucille as a young woman had ridden her horse and gloried in the autumn colors of the
valley. There in the sunshine lay two deep wagon ruts
leading away west.

I laid my rifle in the wild grass and sat on the hard
ground to remove a cactus spine from He-She's black
paw. The dog whimpered softly, then fell silent as we
sat there together gazing out over the valley. In the
distance I could see the red-capped one-hundred-foot
water tower of Ewing shining above the dark treetops
beyond the river. I hadn't seen Gordie for a year. I
wondered if anyone else remembered what I remembered.

- XVII -
Blurry Fragments

Adam Hohman built his barn in 1908. It was huge and straight and white, the barn jewel of the community. For many years, even after it was the Keith Biddlecome barn, people drove out from Ewing to show it to their relatives from out of state.

In my hand I hold a pair of brass-rimmed spectacles with small ovals of flat glass connected by a hand-twisted brass bridge. The primitive temples are nothing more than spring wire bent more than a century ago to wrap around Adam Hohman's ears. With these lenses, he read the Bible aloud to his family every day. His was a stern faith, and when he wired these delicate glasses to his stern face, they seemed as solid as the man himself sitting at the head of the dining room table. They have outlasted him and the sons and daughters who sat attentively around him. They have outlasted the solid Gothic farmhouse too.

An old classmate from my Ewing Elementary School years bought the place in the late eighties. The buildings were useless to him—just the residue of some ancient lives and a sentimental widow who moved to town because she couldn't take care of the place anymore. He sent a Cat out one day to reclaim some useful cropland.

Now I drive north from Ewing, cross the new Elkhorn bridge, and slow my car to a crawl on the quiet county highway. Through the open driver's window, I gaze west to the low bluffs where I once hunted with He-She and scratched in the hard clay where Pawnee braves had once been buried with their war clubs. My view is unimpeded by the wide barn, the creaky farmhouse, the stone chicken coop, the little smokehouse, the antique blacksmith shop, the windmill, the fences and gates, the trees—even the huge lone cottonwood in the corral. Not a splinter of them is left, not a sign. It is as though nothing has ever come out of this land except the corn growing there now tall and shining in the morning sun.

In Ewing old Frank Noffke sits on the bench in front of his blacksmith shop on the south side of Main Street, watching away the summer days with eyes that once saw blacksmith Adam Hohman. As a boy, Frank picked wild grapes out by the river with the old man's granddaughter Lucille. Sold them at a dollar a bushel for wine.

The door behind him stands open to the dim shop which hasn't changed since he apprenticed there for his father, Frank Noffke, Sr., nearly seventy years ago. The thick steel work bench has been hammered thin. The ponderous black lathes and presses and vises look the same as always, standing right where they stand in the early Ewing photographs displayed at Rotherham's Service down on the west corner of the block.

Not much else on Main Street is the same as it was. But Rotherham's still looks the way it did when I was a child. My friend Ed Rotherham took it over from his father and can't bring himself to let go of its past. The old desk in his office is piled with yellowed paper remnants of Ewing's history, and on the north wall hangs an enlarged photograph of Main Street at its zenith in the early fifties.

Frequently Ed strolls down to the blacksmith shop to pick through the historical remnants piled high in Frank Noffke's memory. Together they stare across the street at the gaptoothed old face of Ewing. When Ed and I were children, twelve businesses and a bandstand filled the block on the north side of the street. Now most of those buildings stand empty or not at all. The brick shells of what were once Pollock's Dry Goods and Gibsons' Drug Store are still there at the west end, across from Rotherham's. At the east end, the hair salon and the Eldorado Theater were replaced long ago by scattered weeds.

The remodeled Farmers Bank is still in business, and a feed distributor has erected a metal warehouse in the middle of the block. Its architectural cancer has eaten up several of the false front stores from frontier Ewing—that forgotten Canaan of hopeful pioneers who once crossed the Elkhorn as if it were the Jordan.

Where lines of parked cars once filled the street there are now seldom more than two or three at a time, usually parked near the little franchise grocery that was Ralph's Red and White four decades ago. The festive Saturday nights passed away with the days of family radio and excited hospitality for strangers in town.

From the bench in front of his shop, Frank Noffke can see the old post office on the corner of the next block west and the boarded tomb of the Spittler Brothers general store beside it. As he gazes, there in the street appears the awkward 1917 apparition of Spittlers' open freight truck, now faint, now clear, like Frank's memory. The truck is little more than the heavy rails of a frame supported by open rubber tires and wooden spokes. Its long steering column protrudes from an open engine compartment and, in the angle of Frank's vision, seems to disappear into the rickety wooden crates piled two tiers high behind the driver's bench. Inside the crates are dozens of Chicago Aermotor windmills, the first windmills ever shipped west of the Missouri.

The Spittlers' of Frank's hoary vision is the legendary hardware emporium of the blossoming prairie, once nearly synonymous with Ewing itself. Here the Savidge boys from south of Ewing ordered the engines and other contraptions for their many inventions and eventually for their fabled flying machines which carried them into death and history in the incipient months of aviation. The bosom of every farm and ranch in the surrounding counties still holds pieces of the Spittler enterprise. For half a century, it was the hub of supply for the rivets and gears of progress.

In the other direction from his shop, Frank can see the silver water tower built by John B. Spittler in 1908, still standing in the next block east. Its cap is now green instead of red, and the wooden loading dock beside the alley at its feet exists only in the man-size memories of those of us who as small boys rode up and down its fat planks on fat bicycles and fat ponies.

On a late afternoon in the 1952 autumn of my own memory, Jerry Spangler and I summit the loading dock with a rusty Radio Flyer filled with meat scraps from Ralph's Market. Our mission is to feed Dutch Spangler's redbones, but the coon hounds will have to wait. We pile ourselves on the wagon and rumble together down the ramp, spilling ourselves and the meat into a flourish of Texas sandburs. Our faces contort with laughter until the fear of judgment suddenly falls upon us.

The dock in the sandy alley was abandoned decades ago when Rockeys' Implement and the tile-sided creamery passed away. But the commerce of Ewing isn't all that has passed away. The Presbyterian Church where my dad broke in his shepherd's staff stood a stone's throw from the water tower. In its place now stands the United Methodist Presbyterian Church where Gordon Shrader serves as an elder. It is sanctuary for the combined remnants of families hearing remnants of the gospel that once flourished under two steeples on opposite corners of the intersection. The hopes and hardships and reliance that drew earlier generations to the foot of the cross died with them, and the singular joy of that communion could not be written into their wills for the affluent generation to come.

- XVIII -
Strangers in California

Clayton and I drive slowly north from the Elkhorn Valley in his four-wheel-drive Chevy pickup. The snow-packed road north of Orchard narrows as we enter the steep hills of Verdigre (originally Verdigris) Creek. Beside the road, the snow crystals become a billion diamonds in the afternoon sun.

The hill country is somewhat desolate here, extending on north to the Niobrara. A few farms are scattered through the hollows, but there's no traffic on the winding roads.

"Maybe we shouldn't be coming up here," Clayton suggests. There's hesitation in his voice as well as in his resolve. "I guess it'd be okay not to mention it to Goldie."

The joyous, tumultuous summer of 1964 has turned to winter many times over. Our thoughts crisscross the decades as we continue north, slowly still. Nebraska is brown to the horizon and poured over with white. The ground is hard like stone.

Clayton is fifty now, gray-haired, kids grown. His lifelong ties to the Elkhorn Valley far outnumber my emotional ones. I now live in the mountains of North Carolina—a dozen stops and more than forty years down the tracks from Ewing station. He still lives in the house of his childhood—the house built in 1910 by his grandfather William Hoke, who had homesteaded the place in 1884.

In a narrow hollow we pause beside a fish-hatching pond surrounded by woods rising steeply around us.

Past the pond a sandy road turns east, and we ascend it slowly past the old MacBride house nestled in the trees of the hillside.

Out of the hollow, the incline becomes more gradual for a while, and we follow the little road another mile between barbed wire fences. The grassy hills on both sides are scattered with trees and tied together with snow-covered cow paths.

Before we reach the summit, Clayton stops the truck in the road and turns off the engine. We've been here together before, once, long ago, driving through without stopping. We know that over that sharp crest ahead the road roller-coasters on for a half mile, then curves sharply south through grassland.

A lane leads across the ditch and through an open gate into a hilly pasture. Together we leave the truck, making lines of boot prints in the undisturbed snow through the gate and down to the bottom of a narrow gully. There we stop at a bridge-like concrete culvert, though the lane continues over a frozen creek and up the hill.

We shuffle down the steep bank, and I brush away the snow along the lower sections of the culvert's concrete buttress. We expect to find something, but having never looked before, we are a bit overcome when we do. Little more than a foot from the ground, a chunk of concrete is missing from the smooth surface of the wall south of the culvert opening. It has been gone for three decades, since January of 1965. We stand in the snow, staring quietly. And my mind goes back to the summer of '64.

That summer had seemed eternal. Each new day between high school and college flooded our lives with the exhilaration of new freedom and the anticipation of new discovery. The conflicts and heartaches nourished our hopes as much as did the adventures and passions, for we believed a resolution lay ahead for each one, and there was so much time to discover it. The expectation sometimes squeezed waves of ecstasy from my insides up to my head.

But the summer did end. Gordie went off to join Clayton at the university. I left for college in Iowa. Several teenage girls found new champions to replace us. Nubbins retired to the willow grove west of Grandma Shrader's empty house. Then the winter came, turning summer's exhilarating flood to ice, and jamming our lives with another side of maturation. It was not like the other winters in our lives.

December arrived and I had not been home to California since early summer. I had not seen Gordie since late August. For the first time since that day when I was five years old, I issued him an invitation.

On the first day of Christmas break, I crossed west over the Missouri with several other students in a noisy '56 Chevy. Gordie and Clayton were waiting at a small town near Lincoln. Gordie transferred his suitcase to our trunk and sandwiched himself into the back seat for the trip to the West Coast. We left Clayton waving alone in the cold wind as we sped away down old Highway 30. I watched him turn slowly to Gordie's car for the drive on up the Elkhorn Valley, home.

The confusing excitement of my rendezvous with Gordie was followed by our uncomfortable reacquaintance along the road. More than summer had ended. I longed for a wink across Belva's dining room table, a pillow fight in Gordie's bedroom downstairs, a gallop up the hill from Grandma Shrader's with me holding desperately to the cantle of the saddle. Gordie, I suspected, simply longed to be home on the farm for Christmas.

The long miles west became long, dreary miles, then long, dreary, quiet miles. It seemed that in Gordie's mind they weren't so much leading to Los Angeles as they were leading away from the Elkhorn Valley.

Through the first long night across the Wyoming prairie, the only visible landscape was the narrow highway ahead blurred by clouds of snow driven by the north wind. The drone of the Chevy was at last interrupted on a dark mountain curve near the Utah border. We were descending rapidly along a rocky precipice when we hit ice on the road. The car was out of control in a heartbeat, spinning several times as it continued down the road at high speed. Then, as suddenly as it had started, the spinning and sliding stopped. We found ourselves in the middle of the dark highway, facing Nebraska, frightened and praying together out loud.

During the next day's journey down through Utah and Nevada and into California desert, the emotional burdens of love and life seemed somehow lighter. Our salvation from a potentially deadly plunge had put the more trivial aspects of reality into fresh perspective. But as the face of death faded behind us, our fearful sobriety faded with it. We joked about the driver's skills and even spoke with light-hearted cynicism about the "what ifs" of the night before.

By evening, Gordie was another day further from home and about half that far from me. We simply didn't know each other anymore. Our world had expanded so quickly that the two little boys jumping into the corn bin were only names in a childhood story of a natural son and a stranger passing through. We descended into the L.A. basin with individual sets of regrets.

Our two weeks in Southern California laid out an emotional smorgasbord. For me there was the joy of being home with my family for the first time in six months. But there was also the worry in this familiar setting of my being viewed as the kid I had been before leaving. I feared that no one would ask about my exotic adventures which I would then sagaciously and mysteriously demur from telling. And there was the frustration of Gordie's subdued resentment over being here instead of with his comfortable friends back home, of whom he often spoke. I could have met all these unexpected challenges with grace. But in a perversely immature attempt to win approval, I opted for impudence around my parents and swagger around Gordie. I was disgusting.

The strained relationship with my friend Ken had been forgotten since our split in New York, and he and I agreed to help Gordie realize how glad he was to be in L.A. In the middle of a rainy night during our second week, I lost control of my dad's car on a curve in the Palos Verdes hills. It slid sideways into a low concrete abutment, careened off with two wheels airborne, and hit a stopped car, knocking it into the center of an intersection. The three of us and the lone occupant of the other car were unhurt. My dad's car was injured seriously and the other car critically.

Two days later, Gordie and I were touring the city in the body shop's loaner—a bulbous 1956 Oldsmobile. Not used to driving a car of such dimension, I sideswiped another vehicle, putting a deep crease along the right front fender, both doors, and rear fender of the loaner. Ashamed and terrified of the possible consequences, I gave Gordie the wheel and we cruised up the Long Beach Freeway discussing my immediate options. Gordie was sympathetic to the point of offering to take the rap and filing the accident claim with Farm Bureau back in Nebraska. His offer meant more to me than actually escaping the wrath to come. I asked him to drive me straight to my dad's office at the church so I could make confession.

Dad was remarkably calm and forgiving. That and Gordie's sympathy created one of the few mitigating factors of the whole aggravating holiday. I don't recall what the physical weather was in the following days, but the picture of that time in my mind is always gloomy and cold.

On our long trip back to winter, the banter about driving skills resumed with my recent record as the sole object of humor. The closer we got to Nebraska, the closer the humor got to scorn. Regret for the whole lost vacation was swelling in both of us with obvious tinges of resentment. I had taken Gordie from where he belonged and robbed him of Christmas. And I had assumed a relationship that I had merely crafted out of my own nostalgia.

It was the middle of night when we crossed into Nebraska from Wyoming. By now, the kid who owned the car couldn't keep pace with post-holiday fatigue. Gordie drove the rest of the way across the state, commenting again about my reliability and preempting any possibility of my taking the wheel.

We arrived at the farm midday Sunday, the third of January. There was a polite and exhausted good-bye, and I was off to Iowa, leaving Gordie to pack his own car and go back to the University of Nebraska later that day. That he had so little time to reestablish contact with his local friends seemed the bitter denouement of his California experience. But it wasn't.

The very next Friday, against all time restraints, unneeded expense, hazardous weather, the academic demands of the new semester, and common sense, Gordie picked up Clayton and returned home 150 miles from Lincoln. In subsequent reflection, it seemed foolish and immature. I would have done the same thing.

- XIX -
Tragedy in
the Verdigre Hills

On Sunday afternoon, January 10, 1965, Gordie was packed again, supplied with homemade bread and apple butter, ready to get Clayton and head back to school. At least Belva thought so. But she was being logical. Gordie had last-minute business to attend to in Orchard—business he wouldn't be able to define specifically until he had cruised the five miles to town in his '63 Fairlane. The trip to Lincoln could wait. He had come home for the weekend to retrieve what might be retrievable of his lost Christmas holidays.

On winter Sundays in 1965, a tiny Nebraska town was populated by families at home and perhaps a few young people in cars on the main street. All retail businesses were closed. There were no "convenience" stores, and the only gas station open was at the county seat.

The young people on the street that frigid afternoon included two of Gordie's buddies and two girls from Page, a village northwest of Orchard—girls with whom the boys were no more than acquainted. After a couple of circuits through town and a few minutes of small talk, the five of them were in the Fairlane speeding east on Highway 20.

In circumstances like these, driving into the countryside was less evidence of going than it was of leaving—a symbolic bursting of boundaries—a rite of independence. A few miles out of town they turned north on a frozen dirt road. Somewhere ahead, up west of Verdigre Creek, was "an abandoned road" (as the newspapers later referred to it) that rose and fell through a series of sharp crests—a comfortably long way from California.

Twenty minutes after leaving town, the rite was complete. The Fairlane lay silent and shattered at the bottom of a steep gully in the remote hills north of Orchard—its nose smashed into the wall of a concrete culvert, its rear axle broken, its front suspension unhinged, its four wheels splayed crazily in the snow and dead weeds.

Of the five broken young people inside the car, only Gordie and the girl beside him were conscious. The front seat had been thrust forward over her legs, and she screamed with pain every time he tried to move.

I don't remember who called me long distance from Nebraska. It was probably Gordie's cousin Marilyn, whom I was then hoping to marry and follow into the family. I do remember that northwest Iowa felt colder than ever before.

One bus a day came south from western Minnesota and stopped briefly in front of the small automobile dealership across from the town park. I was waiting in my gray wool coat when it arrived in the late afternoon. Gordie had been taken from the small hospital in Tilden to one of the big hospitals in Omaha, and I was going there because I loved him and because I just realized how much I hated this sanitized little college town.

The bus wheezed south past the Dutch bakery, past the Holland House Cafe, then on south out of town. The sky was choked with gray winter clouds, and the bus was choked with cigarette smoke. Through the front window, I could see nothing but barren cornfields and a ridge of dirty snow scraped up on each side of the highway. It was an ugly place, so very far from

Grandma Shrader's where, at this minute, Gordie and I were five years old and swimming in the stock tank. I was splashing water in his face, and he was loudly cursing me. I had never heard a kid our age say the word he used. But I guess he had never had a preacher's kid splash water in his face.

The bus pulled into downtown Omaha after dark. Squeak Shrader, an older cousin of Gordie's who now lived in Omaha, met me at the bus station and drove me out to the hospital. It was almost closing time.

Gordie was in a room only a short distance from the lobby. When I slipped in, he was lying on his back awake. His pain was as obvious as the black stitches on his face and the cantankerous roommate in the other bed (a man who, in Belva's words, "didn't have a nickel's worth of patience"). Also obvious was Gordie's gratitude for my coming. But behind the obvious was the more profound pain that both of us felt. We were growing up in tragic spurts, and God knew we needed growing.

Several compassionate night nurses provided me with a pillow and blankets and gave me the empty lobby for the night. I lay fully clothed on one of the couches, longing for bygone summers in the Elkhorn Valley. It had been six months since I had sat with my mom on the edge of my own bed in California, trying to tell her why I suddenly wanted to go to New York. She had preempted me. "Life is so short?" she asked softly, looking rhetorically into my eyes. I wasn't prepared for such profundity and was embarrassed to admit I simply wanted to find Brigitta. Suddenly I was groping for wisdom instead of permission. How unsettling to be grown up so soon after graduating from high school. Already I wanted to come home again, and I hadn't even stood up from the edge of my bed, let alone burst the boundaries of seventeen.

My own rite of independence seemed ages past as I now lay in this Omaha hospital down the hall from Gordie's room. Although he would recover with the help of a few steel bones, I realized there in the semi-darkness that he was dying and I was dying. It was not the self-centered nihilism of the sixties settling upon me, but the eternal realism of the Teacher of Ecclesiastes: "Like the fool, the wise man too must die. In days to come both will be forgotten." Whatever either of us had been or would be, whether wise man or fool, it would not fend off our mortality. Whatever either of us had done or would do, whether wise or foolish, it would not matter to generations to come. Immortality was God's doing. And as I listened to the clicking of the lobby clock, I understood clearly now that summer on the Elkhorn truly was not eternal.

The most abrupt crest on that remote road up west of Verdigre Creek was cut down by a bulldozer after the accident. But it demands some slowing down, even today.

After the crash, Gordie had struggled out of the car and climbed up the bank, bleeding into the snow. On the lane above the culvert, he stood staring down at the car and then looking around to get his bearings. He was not far from the road, but he could see that the farmer's pasture gate was closed across the lane. Unless he got help from someone, they all might die.

The parking brake handle had lacerated his left knee, but he had to walk—somewhere. In near delirium, he trudged up the lane north towards the road. He didn't notice his broken arms until his hands refused to open the latch on the gate. He laid the worst arm on the top rail and somehow climbed over. At the road he turned west with no idea how far or even whether there might be a farmhouse. Had he turned east, he and the others would have died that day.

For more than a mile he shuffled along the little road, then down a steep hill into some trees. There were a few buildings nestled into the side of the hill off to his left. It was MacBrides' place. At the house he went into shock.

Dianne Shrader was working at the cafe in Clearwater when Roger Bennett arrived in a panic. Her brother had been in a wreck somewhere north of Orchard. She had to come to the hospital in Tilden right away.

But she couldn't leave just now, she told him. He insisted.

The face she saw in Tilden wasn't her brother's. Yes, it was. They insisted.

Clayton and I climb the slippery bank and stop on the lane over the culvert. For a few moments, we stand with our hands in our pockets, gazing over the edge at our prints in the snow below. Our eyes follow the creek bed away, then crawl up the high hill to the peak in the road an eighth of a mile east.

Thirty years lie between us and that little runaway green Ford. But suddenly we see it appear in the distance. Everything seems normal at first. Then we are terror-stricken. We realize that it's Gordie's car, full of people, and it's out of control. It strips away the barbed wire fence in a bizarre slow motion of exploding snow and wire and wood, launching fence posts in perfect sequence. Then it careens down the long, long hill directly toward us.

- XX -
More Holes in the Wall

The coming of summer 1965 closed our chilly first chapter of college, but the tumult of our incipient adulthood was barely thawing. By now, Gordie's broken arms were healed and his limp far less perceptible than the crash's wintry effect on our lives. Six months after the accident, Gordie seemed to be driving faster, not more cautiously, over the sharp crests of life. To Clayton and me, it was the devil-may-care summer of '64 revisited without innocence.

The sixties road bands from KOMA-IN-OKLA-HOMA, middle America's czar of nighttime radio, paraded with steady beat through Holt and Antelope Counties: The Rumbles, the Starfires, Ray Ruff and the Checkmates, the "fabulous" Flippers. Gordie towed a train of girls successively across the dance floors of both counties, and we caught occasional glimpses.

Clayton and I fancied our behavior to be at least more domestic if not more circumspect. We were inclined to sit in the grass with our girlfriends, Marilyn and Joanie, and watch fireworks at the county fair. How could we explain Gordie's abandon, we all wondered. Had the surgeons in Omaha installed a steel plate in his conscience as well as in his arm? Or was he trying only to drown out sounds from the Verdigre hills?

I worked construction that summer in smalltown South Dakota, living in a cramped upstairs room of an otherwise cavernous old boarding house. The steel bed in the southwest corner took up most of the floor space. A sturdy mission rocker sat beside the head of the bed under a curtained window. A narrow walking space separated the bed from a long dresser with a massive mirror on the north wall. There was another window at the foot of the bed on the south wall.

This room I describe in some detail because of two dreams I had in this place—two dreams remarkably the same. They were not the young-men-shall-dream-dreams type. They were nightmares—begotten, I think now, by the resentments and insecurities of my eighteen-year-old spirit—products of my own careless speed.

From the darkness of a deep trench, I could see light, sunlight, although I could see it only dimly through a narrow opening above me. The trench was like the ones in which I worked daily on the job site. There was planked scaffolding blocking most of the light above my head. In panic I raised my hands to feel for a way out. I had to jump.

My fingers examined the underside of the planking, and it felt remarkably like the ceiling of my room. Standing, I inched carefully along the wall, keeping my eyes on the glimmer of light.

As I crouched to jump, a cloth brushed my arm. In the darkness, I took it in both hands. It felt like a lace curtain—the window curtain beside the foot of my own bed. I awoke within seconds of jumping into the glow of the plate glass mirror.

My heart beat wildly as I lay back down. I hadn't walked in my sleep since childhood, and this had been more than a stroll down the hallway.

A few nights later, the dream came again. There was no curtain this time—just the faint moonlight caught in the tall west window. I braced myself against the wall and jumped hard over the rocking chair to reach it.

Suddenly in my dream, a bottle shattered on the street. Real splinters of glass rained on my bare back. I awoke kneeling on the floor with my face on the edge of the mattress.

Slowly I pushed myself up and flipped the light switch by the door. The curtain was ripped from the window above the rocking chair. The roll-up shade was torn and hung askew from one corner. The top pane was shattered and the screen pushed out. Long blades of glass protruded from the window frame. Bits of glass covered the chair, the floor, the bed.

My cuts and bruises weren't as serious as the emotional tangle beneath the surface. Old Mrs. Martinsen, the landlady, fussed over me with fear in her eyes the next day, suggesting over and over that I go home to my parents in California or "see someone." But I wasn't willing to see even myself—myself kicking holes in the walls of life. I did my best to charm her and offered to pay for the damage to the room. She wouldn't accept a penny.

Images of the dream—the light, the darkness, the desperation to get out—could be tempting fodder for some mystical interpretation, especially since I acted with such determination. But to call these dreams revelatory would be to say only that they were sobering. I was, after all, laboring in trenches during the day. My systems were overloaded with exhaustion and stress. There was nothing really amazing about the images or the sleep-leaping itself.

But there was reason for concern. My expertise in scrutiny was directed always outward. Gordie was too fiery. My classmates were too frozen. The authorities were unjust. The Russians were deceitful. I was daily judging the world from the throne of me. Now my invincibility was beginning to fall on its face. Pushed, I believe, like Dagon.

Gordie and I were one in the emotional turmoil of

our youth, but I was no longer behind him in the saddle. The reins were within my grip as I galloped on toward a farm in a river valley where I would never fully belong. I stared at flawless cowboys in the fading past and only occasionally looked ahead.

- XXI -
Father and Son

Ralph Shrader lost his leg when Gordie was seventeen. For men of less steel, it would have been wholly cathartic. For Ralph, it was a farm crisis to be dealt with after the previous one and before the next one.

He was alone on Grandma Shrader's yard that day grinding feed. He had rigged a car wheel-and-tire as a friction gear to transfer power from the tractor's PTO to the flywheel on the grinder shaft. As he was scooping corn into the hopper, he backed too close to the drive wheel. The spinning tire snatched the leg of his loose jeans.

He was launched into the air, flipped like a coin, and deposited on the ground before he knew his right leg had passed between the tire and the flywheel. The object he had just seen sailing across the barnyard was his own limb.

He crawled to the vacant old house and hoisted himself painfully to the telephone. "I've had an accident," he told Belva without elaborating. He figured they could both do without panic. "Can you come down?"

Belva arrived a few minutes later to find him lying on the kitchen floor. He told her to phone Orchard for the ambulance, then sent her back up to the corner to fetch some aspirin. She also phoned Bennetts and asked Luella to find Roger. When the ambulance arrived, he was there to help load Ralph and his leg.

Reattachment wasn't possible. Ralph spent the Christmas of '63 in the Tilden hospital, that in itself being a personal injury to rival the losing of a leg. He had never been one to spend the night away from home. When he did return to the farm, it was with a thick, straight sock pulled over the sore stump. After it healed, he stuffed it into the top of a plastic calf and went back to work. From then on, he carried a wooden club in the old pickup so he could push the floor starter by hand instead of with his clumsy prosthesis.

It was cancer, not a farm implement, that eventually broke down Ralph Shrader's body. Other more critical parts of his world, however, had been dying for years.

His son, after studying agriculture at the University of Nebraska, had returned to the farm with a wife, a baby, and expectations of partnership and progress. Neither of the latter two was waiting at the door.

As heir, Gordie viewed partnership as the prudent way to prevent inheritance taxes from someday striking like a hailstorm. Ralph wouldn't discuss it. A man's land was to be willed to his offspring, not diluted by the transfers and realignments of corporate legality.

Gordie's enlightened ideas of agricultural progress met similar resistance. By Ralph's assessment, the financial resources of the farm were barely adequate for its own survival, and they would not be gambled on the academic uncertainties of innovation. Gordie hired on with another farmer and moved into an old farmhouse eight miles north of the home place to feed pigs and work someone else's fields. But his desire, his intention, was to till Shrader soil. After several years of "working out," he moved his young family into Grandma Shrader's house, which had stood unoccupied since her death.

Although the move did bring him into a working

relationship with Ralph, it developed slowly, and seeds of tension developed slowly alongside. For Ralph Shrader, half a century of proven ways and means was a heritage nearly impossible to concede, however wanting it might be found. He sat as erect in his saddle of callused experience as he sat in the leather on Nubbins' back.

In Gordie's eyes, however, the old habits of an old farmer were prolonged more by pride than prudence. Old implements with names like eli and lister were rusting in the graveyard behind the willow grove. And the established ways of farmers like Ralph Shrader and Wilbur Bennett were beginning to rust with them. There would soon be no farm at all without the infusion of modern equipment, irrigation, and the latest in agricultural science.

The inevitable changes piled up one by one to create a wagonload of resentment between father and son. But it took years for the blighted fields of their hearts to produce their inevitable harvest of words. The wagon was sturdy and held its frustrated cargo well, spilling over only when rounding the hardest corners.

Ralph's perennial decorum was an attribute of plain Midwestern maturity. He ordered his temperament as he had always ordered his farming, with productive purpose. He noticed everything, took responsibility for it, and didn't mind pointing that out when there was practical necessity to do so.

I'll never forget the day in the summer of 1961 when that decorum ruined my dinner and, thankfully, sealed a page in my conscience for easy reference through decades to come. I had come a long way "out to the farm" this time, since my family had long since moved to Oklahoma. Daddy was on an active duty tour as a chaplain in Korea, and Mother had driven us up through Kansas and Nebraska in the Two-Ten Chevy. With my younger brother and sister, she was spending her long vacation visiting Lucille at the Biddlecome farm down by the river. I chose to spend as much time as I could "working" with Gordie at Shraders'.

On that particular morning, he and I were to move some rye to the elevator. For in those days, Elkhorn Valley farmers sowed rye and vetch in their cornfields to enrich the soil.

Gordie left Grandma Shrader's yard first, pulling a full wagon with the M. I jumped in the old green pickup which was mounded high with rye. My interest, however, was not so much in hauling grain as it was in catching Gordie on the tractor. I was too young for a driver's license but old enough to thrill at the response of a throttle. I punched the old six, carved an arc in the hard sand in front of the barn, and bounced heavily between the cottonwoods and onto the road, oblivious to the long-established fact that Ralph Shrader noticed everything of relevance to his farm. And I had left a message plain enough for the horses to read.

Several men from the haying crew showed up for dinner that day, and Belva's dining room table was piled high with food. Not high enough, however, to hide a skinny kid from Oklahoma. "Someone came hellin' outa that yard with the pickup," Ralph announced. "Slung off six bushel of rye." I stared at my plate, wishing I'd stayed at Biddlecomes'. Gordie stared at his plate too, loyally saying nothing, yet communicating clearly to me, "You're not really a farmer."

I was impressed that Ralph knew; more impressed that he knew how many "bushel"; most impressed that the word "hellin'" had crossed his lips. He had been an elder in my dad's church.

It was also, I noted, the only time I had ever heard hell used as a verb.

Gordie and I were fourteen that summer. Since we had outgrown noonday naps, we regularly carried our

.22s down to the barn to shoot pigeons off the roof while Ralph snoozed on the living room rug. Sometimes we sneaked up the ladder into the haymow and shot them off the rafters. Belva even fried some up for us once, and we gnawed at them proudly.

Tottering weak-kneed on the verge of collapse, the old barn still stands today by Ralph's little house up at the corner. It would be risky to climb into the haymow to see the tines of light silently betraying the bullet holes in the roof. There might not be any roof at all by now had Ralph not taken notice and put an end to our pigeon hunting. We were forced to take up rat hunting.

In later years, when Gordie was a man, those unavoidable occasions of Ralph's pointing things out exacerbated his frustrations with what he interpreted to be his father's aversion to progress. Ralph's frequent observations seemed to have shifted from matters of practical necessity to matters of preference. Gordie's negative reactions began as offhand contradictions, then slipped into cynicism and eventually into open condescension.

Even so, Ralph bore a nonverbalized pride in his son and in his own apparent legacy of accomplishment. From time to time, it flushed his weathered cheeks. But he refused to admit any practical purpose in allowing it to go beyond that point. And the joy was sapped by the perception of his gradual and inextricable demotion to the hired hand on his own farm. He was no longer the leader of his people. And he sometimes felt little respect for having been.

Ralph Shrader had grown with the land for nearly seventy years. Whatever could happen on a farm, in plenty or in want, he had known. He was not opposed to progress. Had he not—under the raised eyebrows of his own father—moved long ago from horse team to tractor?

There were, however, things in life that didn't change. And by his reckoning, the basic ways of dealing with them didn't change either.

- XXII -
Longing for Intimacy

Ralph was the eldest of six children, first following his father, then walking beside him, then taking over the farm and indefatigably nurturing it to maturity. He was a decision maker, and good enough. That was his domain. That and the Shrader farm. And as he met the challenge, he believed it was seldom expedient to consult even his wife. How hard it would be to surrender that ascendancy.

"He didn't tell us a lot of things," was Belva's tearfully cryptic way of recounting, years later, a history of circumspect seclusion. It had become difficult for her to see that it was a seclusion shared equally on either side of an intellectual and emotional screen door. Through the summers and winters of their circumspection, they had silently reached out for intimacy—until they embraced the silence itself as its fulfillment. It was an enduring weakness they came to mistake for enduring strength.

Before the cancer had its way, Ralph broke the silence one evening, softly, remorsefully. "Gordie was mean to me today," he told Belva. It was not so much a report or a revelation as it was, at last, his simple confession of mortality, of unavoidable emotion.

It came years too late. Belva's cup was simply too full of her own emotional frustration to hold what she desperately wanted. "Shut up! Just shut up!" she cried. And the house was silent again.

For thirteen years after Ralph's death, she mourned over that moment, not recognizing the obvious until the final weeks of her own life. She wept when she told me she had not been there for him when he needed her the most. And after the tradition of their antiphonal silence, she had never reconciled that regret with either Ralph or herself.

For all those years, she never understood that nothing she might have said that night would have revealed so clearly the depth of her love for him. How could she know that Ralph did see it—finally vulnerable and finally able to realize his long entrenched blindness not only to Gordie's dreams but to her anguish? If only he had cultivated the joys of their faithful love with the same vigor with which he had cultivated his corn and his self-sufficiency.

It was the beginning of the adult stage of his metamorphosis, the shedding of a cocoon of antiquated assumptions about manhood, grown thick with years.

Ralph's first date with Belva had been an impromptu performance during the summer of 1935, broaching the overwhelming reticence which blessed them both. The American nation was beset that summer by economic depression. But for young men like Ralph Shrader and Dewitt Hoke, that was only the America in the radio. The other America, the America of the upper Elkhorn, was beset by thrashing. It was like every other year in their memories. Corn was worth only ten cents a bushel, eggs five cents a dozen, but the only thing akin to depression was the anxious thought of missing the county fair in Neligh. Thrashing provided them less opportunity for "chumming together" than for working together.

When an open evening appeared, Ralph agreed to take his car. He cleaned up in a hurry and swung around the section to pick up Dewitt. When they met Belva at the fair that night, Ralph relieved her girlfriends of her company and appointed Dewitt his official chauffeur.

Ralph and Belva were married in March, 1936 and remained childless for eight years. "Can I go up to Dr. Gordon?" she asked him in 1944—not to plead but to confirm their mutual resolve to seek adoption. Dr. Gordon Fletcher in Orchard had ties with the Nebraska Home for Children in Omaha. With Ralph's blessing, she went to town.

Before she could explain the reason for her visit, Dr. Gordon surprised her: "What would you think about adopting a child?"

Ralph was in the field when the case worker came up the following month from Omaha. Belva brought her out along a sandy lane where they waited for the tractor to make another round. Ralph climbed down from his rig and politely greeted their guest with a long smile and his customary short sentences. They told her they wanted a girl.

When the notice of an available nine-month-old girl arrived later, Ralph and Belva left the yard early one morning and drove to Omaha. They arrived at the Home for Children before noon only to meet disappointment. The child they had come to see, they agreed, was not meant for them. The case worker suggested that they get something to eat and return to the Home in the afternoon. When they did, there was a three-month-old baby girl waiting in the consultation room. They named her Dianne.

Dianne was two when Belva went to see Dr. Gordon again, with Ralph this time. They wanted a son. Again they drove to Omaha, and when they arrived, there was little time for reflection or doubt. As soon as the two-month-old baby boy was bundled in to meet them, Dianne cut to the quick. "Let's go home."

"So we did," Belva said later. It was spring, 1946. She and Ralph named their new son Gordon Wayne after Dr. Fletcher, who had "delivered" him and after the two Uncle Waynes who had prayed for him.

Forty-nine years later, Gordon Wayne Shrader returned to Omaha with his mother. This time, he was cradling instead of being cradled. She was in his arms, small and helpless. "Open your eyes and look at the fields," the Lord of harvest had told her often from the pages of her large-print Bible. "They are ripe." Now he was gathering Belva herself into eternity. It was spring, 1995. On Good Friday, Gordie came home without her. The flowers were not yet blooming.

"They're waiting for Easter," our dear North Carolina mountain friend Miss Lula used to tell us before she died. "Jesus must rise from the grave. Then the flowers will bloom." Miss Lula was waiting for Belva, I'm sure, with an embrace and an unwilting Easter bouquet.

Clayton called me first, long distance. We spoke with controlled sorrow. The emotion didn't spill until I talked with Gordie. During her last two days of life in the hospital in Omaha, Belva had tried to tell him something she had waited too long to say. She struggled to force words beyond her pneumonia and her final frailty. But she could not break through. Gordie tried to steady her hand on a chalk slate. She scribbled desperately, but it was only scribble. "It's okay, Mom," he said to comfort her.

"No, it's not," she whispered with the last of her breath. Again it was too late for words. But there was no need to explain anything—to Gordie—or to Ralph. It was okay.

- XXIII -
The Dark Canvas

During my first student years in Iowa, I fled my academic responsibilities whenever I could—in every season. I was lost—a California outsider in an ethnic county, ethnic town, ethnic school—unneeded, unwelcome, disconsolate, afraid of what others in the daunting society of college expected me to be. That darkness drove me away. I longed to dye my hair black like Elvis or sleep in a coffin like James Dean. But I suppressed such noble sentiments of rebellion with the self-inflating assumption that they would be wasted on such a sterile culture.

Other students were routinely homesick, timid, indecisive, lonely. It was college, after all. Some of them have perhaps written memoirs about their own alienation and agony in those years, but, at the time, I refused to recognize the depth in those around me. I selfishly distanced myself from them, pacing the perimeter of friendships like a coyote pacing the shadows of Biddlecome's yard light with the sanctuary of the Elkhorn nearby.

Whenever I hitchhiked west out of Iowa, I peeled off layers of anxiety at every crossroads. I stood beside highways, sometimes for hours in cold rain or blowing snow, shivering more from bitter introspection than from bitter cold. I believe now that I wanted to suffer as a confirmation of manhood in my quest for boyhood reclaimed.

The inner struggles of those years fluctuated like weather and faded with my youth. I had no idea that

inner struggles of far greater duration and conse-
quence were raging within Gordie's family—the very
people in whom I found respite. Belva's emotional
isolation from Ralph was slowly driving her to mental
collapse. A bitter root of darkness was growing on
Shrader land.

Time is a canvas on which the spirit paints. The
strokes of the brush are sometimes subtle and sometimes bold, and the colors soften and flow from the
prism of men's tears in the evening sun. They blend and
turn and glisten in the light and fade. And the struggles
of the spirit become a landscape on the canvas. The
breath of heaven cools the tears and dries them in
shining paths on men's faces. The landscape is, at last,
a portrait sitting on an old piano.

In my youth, I never saw the full portrait of the
Shrader farm in all its darks and lights. Many brush
strokes were revealed only after those parts of the canvas were finished, years later. As the colors of Gordie's
life seemed to grow rich with both sunshine and
shadow, invisible strokes in Belva's life darkened her
world. It now seems ironic that on the Shrader farm in
those same years I found light for the dark corners of
my life. Belva was a mother to me in the college years
when I was so far from my own family. I never saw the
darkness in her.

Seeds of her eventual collapse appeared early in
Gordie's life, a kind of possessive grip that might have
been precluded by Ralph's intimate embrace. By the
time her grandchildren came along in the late sixties,
she was overwhelmed with anxiety. She phoned
Ralynn, Gordie's wife, several times a day to check on
the grandchildren. She badgered her own daughter,
Dianne, with fearful remonstrance about how she was
raising her kids. The rest of the time, she fretted back
and forth through the house as if she were late for an
appointment.

Her psychoses drove the whole family crazy, until in the mid-seventies Ralph finally drove her the fifty miles to the state hospital at Norfolk. She stayed for eight weeks, forced to supplant her own unwanted advice with the unwanted advice of psychiatrists. She told Lucille Biddlecome, who worked there at the time, that she had never thought she'd end up living with crazy people. She didn't see much hope in it.

Two months of group therapy apparently confirmed her apprehensions, although she didn't see it that way. She was trained to speak her mind openly instead of penting up her emotional turmoil. She apparently graduated *summa cum laude* and went home to apply the trendy psychology of the seventies. The compulsive behavior that had been so annoying for years had been subdued. A new behavior was in place.

Belva spoke her mind—to her family, to the store clerks, to the ladies' society at church. The unsettling anxiety that had been an annoyance was now an embarrassment and often an offense, alienating people in the community and members of her own family. The experts in Norfolk had led her to believe she would find healing through her new candidness—which she saw as confessional. When she found quite the opposite, she became more confused, and the bitter root grew.

- XXIV -
Back to the Elkhorn

A small, white Grumman Cheetah drones slowly southwestward over the verdant cornfields and stately cottonwoods of Nebraska. In the pilot's seat is my lifelong friend Gordon Shrader, and I sit beside him.

We are headed back to the farm after flying to Sioux Falls for the repair of a computerized seeder control unit. As South Dakota fades into the rear horizon, the corduroy of row crops yields to the tweed of the sparsely inhabited hills of Verdigre Creek. In a little while, we will cross into Antelope County, and in a blink of time, our shadow will darken the scarred concrete culvert beside a lonely road somewhere below.

"Wanna take it?" Gordie shouts over the noise of the single engine. "Wanna fly for a while?"

I am reluctant, but I clutch the yoke and manage to stabilize the thing after wobbling around the sky for the first few minutes. "I never thought I'd do this!" I shout. But my words are true only in the particular of flight. For in the universal of our relationship, I have done this before—appeared briefly to put my hand to the yoke of Gordie's life, to wobble along beside him, then to disappear again into some world beyond the Elkhorn Valley.

It has now been more than forty years since my first disappearing, when I followed my father away down Highway 275 to the rest of my growing up. In my child's grieving heart, I could not then fathom the depth of that channel cut through it by the waters of the Elkhorn.

On the July morning in 1955 when our '50 Ford rolled out of Ewing and over the South Fork bridge for the last time, I actually wanted nothing more than to hurry on. Hidden under the bridge was an open pack of cigarettes my friend Larry and I had stolen from his father's beer joint. I was eight.

In the broad light of a summer afternoon, we had walked right through the front door and into my first conscious experience of the hell my dad so often preached about. There wasn't a soul in the place, lost or otherwise. We slipped past the shuffleboard table and reached a pack of Lucky Strikes from high above the dark wooden counter on the wall behind the bar. My heart pummeled my lungs like punching bags as we crept back out the door and ran breathless down the wide sidewalk past Mrs. Eggelston's Variety and Frank Noffke's blacksmith shop, past the old pool hall, and around the corner at Emmet Wright's Repair. I was convinced that I had stepped beyond the fiery brink and was now headed for the real hell where smokers and drinkers go when they die.

The confirmation came when the Sisson boys caught us smoking under the bridge and threatened to tell my father, the preacher.

Now as I watched the water tower shrink in the distance behind the Ford, my eyes were peeled for Sissons. I imagined my dad someday coming back here from Oklahoma to find out, and my heart started pounding again.

All those fears faded before the arrival of my ninth birthday later that year. By fall, going back to the Elkhorn Valley had become my highest priority. In October, I received a letter from Ewing with a small black-and-white photo labeled "School Days 55-56." On the back I penciled in staggering cursive, beginning with a small letter, "this is the best pal in the world—Gordon Shrader," then slipped the picture tenderly into my Randolph Scott billfold.

Gordie again has control of the Cheetah. We descend toward Orchard, coming in low over the graveyard east of town, where a polished, brown gravestone stands back toward the shelter belt away from the road. The image of its simple west edifice is chiseled in my mind with the large letters "SHRADER" and the smaller words "Ralph" and "Belva" under them.

The sun lights up the white wings of the airplane as we bank toward Ewing for a couple of nostalgic turns around the old town. Then before touching down at Gordie's landing strip north of the farm, we glide low along the river in the evening sun. Our shadow flickers over the golden banks, and suddenly I am lost in another time, looking down at the preacher's family having a Sunday picnic in the trees south of Gunters'. There I stand beside the river, ageless and staring at images in the water.

Just upstream west of Gunters' my hand-me-down brown bike is lying beside my clothes in the sand under the old county bridge. I'm there too with several other naked seven-year-olds, listening for cars approaching the bridge. It's June, 1954, and it's my turn. At the sound of a vehicle, I run into the open, jump up and down and wave my arms as the car crosses the river, then dash back for a victory jump into the deepest hole in the shallow water.

A couple of miles downstream it's August, 1954. I'm splashing through the shallow river with my father, chasing carp onto sandbars and grabbing at wild gold-fish in the warm, clear water. It's an exciting moment having him here with me. He takes me bullhead fishing in country ponds and .22 shooting out at the dump. But I bring him here, even though he doesn't know it. At seven years old, I know the Elkhorn better than he. My childhood is one of adventure. This is my river.

The gravel pit is just downstream from the

Gunters' place, on the same side of the river. From the deepest pond, an overflow channel about ten feet wide has been dug to the river. Only a trickle of water flows between its high vertical banks. It's summer, 1961. Somewhere between the river and the pit there's a terrible commotion between the banks of the channel. Three horses have sunk into quicksand. They are frenzied, screaming and snorting.

Smokey's rear quarters are down. Clayton is off ahead on solid ground, jerking at the reins. Behind Smokey, Nubbins is floundering on his side in the quicksand with me still on his back. My right leg is trapped under him, and Angel has keeled over on my left leg. Gordie has slid off to the left and is tugging frantically to get Angel up. All six of us figure we're going to die.

The three horses are wrong. They will arrive home with nothing worse than a hard coat of muck up to their withers. Dewitt will welcome Clayton home with his usual leathery amiability. As for Gordie and me, Ralph is going to kill us.

Upstream beyond the county road, on Biddlecomes' land, I'm a college boy walking with a squirrel gun among the cottonwoods north of the river. I pick a musk turtle out of a green swamp, kick sand away from a coyote den in the riverbank, follow deer tracks across a sandbar. It's early spring, 1966. Gordie is in Lincoln at the university. He'll be married come summer, and on his wedding night, the Ewing sheriff will haul Clayton and me to the jail at the firehouse simply for celebrating the youthful blessing of bachelorhood.

Now Clayton is away too, studying agriculture at the university. I sit down among the wild grasses on the river's north bank, propping my rifle against a tree. The Elkhorn lies before me in the quiet of the valley, shallow again after the early spring runoff. Like our lives, it flows away unchecked.

Yet the river doesn't change like those of us crossing over it. Our childhood is gone. I'll never go "out
to the farm" again, even though I'll come back to it
year after year. I'll never live in a world as small or as
poor or as secure as the Elkhorn Valley I knew. It was
a child's world. My Ewing friends of long ago—
tongue-tied Terry, crazy Lonnie, slow Louie, shy Robert, wide-eyed Jerry—are, who knows, long gone
somewhere, no longer ragged and immortal.

I've hitchhiked from Iowa for a weekend of Belva's
white bread and apple butter, of riding ol' Nubbins
bareback across the hayfields, of sitting alone on the
banks of this sand-bottom river, remembering.

I'm close to God here. He knows this sadness in-
finitely better than I. "Remember him," says the
Teacher, "before the silver cord is severed." The
meaningless—the finite which I hold so dear—is slip-
ping through my fingers, and I weep at the loss. Under God's breath, the petals of the flowers are falling.
Otherwise I would hold on forever to nothing more
than grass.

As I gaze from the airplane across the dusky valley, I
find myself in a silent house, staring motionless
through a closed window into a moonless night. I've
just read the last page of a novel, and I'm full to the
throat with the emotion of its passing. I tell myself that
this awful fullness, this emptiness, will also pass.

Then in the darkness of the glass I discern the
twinkle of a solitary yard light on a distant farm.

-XXV -
The Death of Ralph Shrader

In the mid-seventies, when the discord between Ralph and Gordie was at a crescendo, there was no airplane. The rest was the same—my occasional visits from somewhere, my brief attempts at copiloting Gordie's life, our brief intimacies of conversation and laughter, our forays into nostalgia. In material terms, the concerns of those days on Ralph's small farm were modest. In emotional terms, they were greater than the wide corporate enterprise that is today the Gordon Shrader Farms.

On one of those visits, the long impasse over the future of Shrader land had brought Gordie to a state of depression and anger. He believed that Ralph's stubborn refusals of partnership were destined to shut him out altogether, and he had come to interpret his father's deep conviction as rejection. Instead of opening up to each other, they had closed up.

In impetuous desperation, Gordie acceded to my presumptuous offer of mediation, and I went up to Ralph's one evening to put things on the table.

There I sat like the stranger I was, facing Ralph and Belva in their fifties-green living room. They were not only willing to accept my intrusion, but quite willing to get to the point. Several points, as it turned out. Gordie wondered about their love for him. "Does he also wonder if adoptive parents love their children?" Belva asked from somewhere near the surface of her patience. I realized that the consequences of spilling Ralph's rye out of the pickup when I was a kid had been nothing compared to the consequences of spilling my arrogance on the living room floor. In this matter, Ralph and Belva were one, and there was no uncertainty about their mutual preparedness. Ralph's sandy voice harmonized with Belva's paved one, and they spoke more firmly as the subject of Gordie's sister, Dianne, became part of the equation. They expressed their conviction that it would be wrong somehow to favor Gordie with the assets of the farm. And they confessed their perennial anguish over the lawsuit that had hung around their necks since his 1965 car wreck. The girl beside him in the front seat had been paralyzed for life. For years now, Ralph and Belva had expected to lose the Shrader farm. They felt rejected.

"And Gordon feels rejected?" Belva told me, for it was a question being told, not asked. She was not putting the emphasis on the second syllable of Gordie's name as I was used to hearing.

By June of 1980, Gordie's desperation had risen from the pit of his stomach to his heart, and the issues of land had collapsed under matters of love. Ralph had been diagnosed with cancer, and Gordie was stricken with grief and regret.

He called me at my hospital bed in Rochester, Minnesota, where I was recovering from major surgery under the auspices of the Mayo Clinic. Now in a deeper sense, he was desperate over his relationship with Ralph, overwhelmed with fear and convictions of unworthiness. Simply, he wanted his father and didn't know how to embrace him. He asked me to come.

My wife, Carol, and I lived in Kansas at the time, but we headed for Nebraska, willing to give and wondering how. I wanted to be a friend this time, not an intruder. All I had was an open ear and the most

obvious advice I could muster. Few conflicts of any
duration cannot be neutralized by the words "I'm
sorry." And forgiveness heals even the most jagged
wounds of our regret. What's right is usually so
simple.

As Gordie confessed to me his deep love for
Ralph, he confessed also that he had never just told
him straight out, "I love you." My only counsel was
that he say it—and do it. Honor thy father. That was
the clear command he had contravened. It was hard
counsel.

Ralph lived two more years with open lines of
communication. That is, open lines of love. The daily
priorities for both father and son became radically
different. It was no confirmation of my advisory wisdom. I had been there only to listen as Gordie talked
himself out of his dear accumulation of grief, although
he wept easily and frequently for the next two years.

In Ralph's final week, Gordie took him to Omaha in
the desperate hope of rolling back the ravages of the
cancer. But there was nothing more that could be
done there. The doctors sent him home. The disease
had climbed from his prostate into his neck, and the
pain was almost unbearable, even for Ralph Shrader.
To compound the misery, a tumor at the back of his
neck had been treated with radiation through the
mouth. His sense of taste was now gone, and even his
ability to swallow diminished to the point that he
could hardly eat even to please his own son who tried
patiently to spoon-feed him.

The decades of bare practicality were over, and the
heartgates had swung open on their rusty hinges. The
conflicts they had both cultivated into rancor were
past. The crops, the machines, the stiff-necked si-
lences, the markets, the weather, and the land itself
were behind.

Several times on the trip from Omaha back to

Ewing, Gordie had to stop along the road to help Ralph get out and drape his gaunt body over the car. There he massaged his father's back and neck with a weight of tenderness far greater than the weight of verbal abuse he had once heaped upon those straight shoulders.

The physical descent from there was rapid. Ralph spent that night at home, but his needs were greater than Belva's ability to meet them. Gordie came up in the morning and rolled him to the car in a wheelchair for the final trip to the Tilden hospital. "It's Molly's turn to be in the pasture," Ralph told him. Molly had been part of his favorite team in the thirties when hitches were rotated from barn to pasture. His mind had remained strong to the end, and this was the end.

Ralph's last day was a Sunday in the middle of June, 1982. Gordie was in town at the Lunch Box after church when Belva phoned him from the hospital in Tilden. "I think Gordie will want to see me," was all Ralph had told her.

Belva and Dianne were asleep in the waiting room when Ralph died that night. Gordie was in Ralph's room on the bed next to his father's. "I love you, Dad," he said before they fell asleep together.

When the long-distance call came from Gordie's wife, Ralynn, an image from my childhood appeared before me. Ralph was standing in the bathroom just off the farmhouse kitchen, washing up for dinner. I could see the rolled-up sleeves of his blue shirt, his white scrubbed arms, his powerful brown hands. The market report from Yankton drifted in from the living room radio, and the aroma of Belva's fresh white bread filled the room.

- XXVI -
Faint Echoes of the Farm

The old barn at Grandma Shrader's place lived longer than the house. To me that barn was always the crown of the farm. I miss it more than all the rest, even more than the willow grove back by the old schoolhouse where Nubbins used to stand and whisk away flies in the summer shade.

The barn's peaked roof sloped down north toward the road and more gradually down on the south end toward the corral where Gordie and I rode sows when Ralph was in the field. The farrowing room was there in the south end. The tank where we watered the horses was just outside at the southwest corner. When we were little, it was the best place to dismount with the help of the board fence beside it.

The horse stalls, tack room, and stairs to the haymow were in the middle section under the peak. Huge sliding doors opened both to the east and to the west, creating a breezeway between the rows of stalls. The stall dividers were about horse high, and the thick top plank of each was scalloped by half a century of horse gnawing. Here we curried and picked cockleburs and cinched up saddles. When Gordie was as young as five, he always knew when a horse was puffing its belly against the cinch. I was awed to see such a huge beast submit to Gordie's little boot, groaning briefly in disgust and then sighing its belly down to size.

In those early years, we had to climb the stall to get into the saddle, then duck our heads as the horse went through the wide doorway and took the jolting first step down from the barn's high foundation.

In the north end of the barn were two large paddocks with straw-covered floors and Dutch doors. Here Ralph sat on a battered peg-leg milking stool with his head bowed into the flank of a cow. Here he taught me how to milk by hand and how to squirt a white arch into a cat's face. When I was a teenager, I even pulled a few pails myself. Here Angel foaled for the first time and here her black colt spent his first days of life.

A large new brick house now sits on a knoll twenty yards west of the place where Ralph Shrader was born. From the front porch I look east over a low brick fence surrounding a manicured lawn. Beyond its wrought iron gates is sunshine and sand and grass growing where the old house was. I watch the end tower of a pivot system roll slowly through the cornfield. The spray from its end gun reaches the crop growing where the barn once stood. Then the tower passes through its own rainbow in the afternoon sun. It soaks the spot where Ralph's shop huddled under a tree west of the windmill.

Straight out across the yard, the old drive-through granary still stands near the road directly north of the barn site. Gordie and I played barefoot there in the cool corn, while our parents sat visiting around the Sunday dinner table up at the corner. The wooden granary is now nothing but an antique backdrop for family photographs. The corn not already sold from Gordie's 5,600 acres of irrigated crop is stored in huge steel granaries lined up behind the new house.

Grandma Shrader's house was gone long before the Bennett place up the road disappeared. The fence, the gate, and the arthritic elms in the front yard went with it. So did Ralph's cluttered shop out back, where I first breathed the muscular aroma of men and grease and cut steel. The low chicken coop beside the shop was cleared away too and buried with everything else. It had been nearly forgotten anyway. There hadn't been any chickens in it for years, and it lay hidden by wild marijuana and sunflowers.

The large concrete cistern was dozed too. It had stood for close to a century in the center of the barn-yard, its tall, shingled roof-cone hunched by the weight of years.

The house itself had stood empty, season upon season after May Shrader's death. The men continued to warm themselves by its old oil stove in winter and refresh themselves in summer with its sweet Nebraska water. They stored their livestock vaccines in the refrigerator and used the telephone for farm business and emergencies.

When Gordie came home with his young family in the late sixties, he and Ralynn made it a home again—even added on and gave the old place some color. In the early eighties, he burned it all down and buried the rubble beneath the footprints of five generations. Rubble is the wrong word. Rubble is the residue of old wood, linoleum rugs, plaster walls, solid doors, flawed window glass, and iron pipe. This fire burned more than that.

Faint echoes of laughter and crying and a billion words went down with these walls. The souls of people were molded like clay in this place. They shook hands here and embraced here. They came into the world here, suffered, made love, solved problems, rejoiced, sobbed, and gulped their last air. They planned and prayed and comforted each other and argued and lay awake at night with pounding hearts.

They came home here. They read books and held secrets and taught their children of seeds and sorrow. They watched their crops grow in the summer and took shelter from blizzards in the winter.

This fire, this burial—they were more than Shrader. They were Bennett and Gunter and Biddlecome and Hoke and countless other families summed up in a few yellowed papers and gravestones.

Farmer Job had seen this vanity from his own ash heap thousands of years earlier. Like these families, he had seen the miracles of creation, the waters suspended in the clouds, the quaking pillars of the heavens, the skies blown clear by the breath of God. All of it, he declared, was "but the outer fringe of God's works. How faint the whisper."

The miracles of this land, the seed time and harvest, even the lives of these strong people, were faint whispers that dropped into silence. How meaningless, says the Teacher. "Even the memory of them is forgotten. Never again will they have a part in anything that happens under the sun."

How meaningless to toil for the wind. Meaningless, except in the thunderous hope that sustained Job in his mourning. Like the faithful dead of the Elkhorn Valley, he had heard the thunder of the High King crossing the skies on the white horse of heaven.

He had looked beyond the whispers of the childhood I could never reclaim—to a perfect Nebraska valley with a crystal river flowing from God's throne and eternally out through flowered pastures and cottonwoods.

Our God, our help in ages past,
our hope for years to come:
O be our guard while troubles last,
and our eternal home.